*Mother Claudette,
Thanks for your support! You are a Blessing!*

RIVERS OF LIFE
A COLLECTION OF LIFE-CHANGING SERMONS AND HOMILIES

Kendra T. Davis

"Out of your BELLY shall flow RIVERS of living water!"
John 7:38 KJV

Copyright © 2012 by Kendra T. Davis
All rights reserved. Except as provided by the Copyright Act of 1976. No part of this publication may be reproduced, stored in a retrieval system or transmitted in any form or by any means without the prior written permission of the publisher.

Unless otherwise noted, all Scriptures are from the Holy Bible, New Living Translation, copyright © 1996. Used by permission of Tyndale House Publishing, Inc. Wheaton, Illinois 60189. All rights reserved.

Scriptures noted KJV are taken from the KING JAMES VERSION of the Bible. Scriptures noted NIV are taken from the NEW INTERNATIONAL VERSION of the Bible.

Published by:
MAC PUBLISHING
www.macpub.org

RIVERS OF LIFE
ISBN-10: 0985027762
ISBN-13: 978-0-9850277-6-6

TABLE OF CONTENTS

DEDICATION **4**

HONORABLE MENTIONS **6**

INTRODUCTION - DISCOVERING THE GOD IN ME **8**

THE NILE RIVER-"FAITH" **10**

DROP THE CHARGES 11
STEPPING OUT! 14
SPEAK THE WORD 17
I'M IN PROTECTIVE CUSTODY 20
USHER ME INTO THE PRESENCE OF THE LORD! 24
EXPECTING A RIDICULOUS BLESSING 25
THERE IS A MIRACLE IN YOUR MOUTH 29

THE RIVER OF SIHON- "POWER & AUTHORITY" **31**

I GOT THE POWER 32
IT'S MINE & I WANT IT BACK! 36
THE INTERRUPTION OF EVERYTHING 39
I SEE YOU... Don't Quit! 44
WALKING IN THE POWER OF NOW! 45
FACE OFF: DEALING WITH THE REAL ME! 49
I DECLARE WAR! 53

THE JORDAN RIVER- "EXHALTATION" **56**

YOU'RE NOT TRASH BUT TREASURE 57
THE MAKING OF A CHAMPION 59
I AM A COMEBACK KID! 62
A PECULIAR PEOPLE 66
IT'S POSSIBLE SERIES: 68
    RISE UP! 68
    MY LIFE IS CHOICE-DRIVEN 70
    I CHANGED MY MIND. HE RESTORED ME! 71

IDENTIFY YOUR PURPOSE 73
YOUR RIGHT TO EMPOWER YOUR BELIEF 74
ENGAGE IN SPIRITUAL WARFARE: FIGHT! 77

THE RIVER EUPHRATES – "PROVISION" 80

I'M STEPPING INTO MY CHANGE 81
THE GREAT INVESTMENT 83
GO TO YOUR WEALTHY PLACE 86

THE RIVER OF EGYPT – "PROMISES" 91

PREGNANT WITH A PROMISE 92
THE PROCESS: MARY'S PROMISE 94
    PRINCIPLE ONE: CALM DOWN! 94
    PRINCIPLE TWO: STAND IN FAITH! 95
    PRINCIPLE THREE: STUDY TO BE QUIET! 96
    PRINCIPLE FOUR: WORK! 97
    PRINCIPLE FIVE: BEWARE OF YOUR SURROUNDINGS!
    97
    PRINCIPLE SIX: POSITION YOURSELF! 98
    PRINCIPLE SEVEN: FIGHT FOR IT! 98
    PRINCIPLE EIGHT: PUSH! 99
    A PROMISE IS STILL A PROMISE! 100

THE AMAZON RIVER – "RELATIONSHIPS" 102

I HAVE A FATHER! 103
NOT YOUR AVERAGE WOMAN! 105
THE COMPANY THAT YOU KEEP 107
DATING 101 109
SINGLE AFTER GOD'S OWN HEART 114

ABOUT THE AUTHOR 116

CORRESPONDENCE 118

DEDICATION

It is with great pleasure that I dedicate this book, "***Rivers of Life***" to my spiritual parents, Bishop Sheldon M. McCarter and Co-Pastor Joyce McCarter.

Ephesians 6:1-3 declares: "Children, obey your parents in the Lord: for this is right. Honor thy father and mother; (which is the first commandment with promise) that it may be well with thee, and thou mayest live long on the earth."

I am a living testimony of these scriptures. As your spiritual daughter of sixteen years, the two of you have imparted and invested so many great things into my life. Like any parents, you have encouraged me when I was right and had no problems correcting me when I was wrong. I am so thankful that the two of you had the courage to tell me the truth with love and offer sound wisdom and guidance. God could not have entrusted my life into the hands of a better couple. The opportunity to sit and to serve under your leadership has allowed me to grow and become the woman of God that I am and has given me the necessary tools to be a change-agent, making a difference in the kingdom of GOD.

As I embark upon my eighth year in ministry, I wanted to take the time to personally and publicly thank you for all the investments you have made in my life. I appreciate the times you have allowed me to hold your answering machine hostage as I preached my sermons and patiently awaited your feedback before going out to preach.

One of the greatest investments I believe you have made in making me the anointed and effective preacher that I am is the process of waiting. I remember coming to you, expressing the call of GOD on my life and your words were, "I don't doubt that at all! When God releases me, I will release you!" Many see the glory but they don't know the story! I waited five years before you released me into ministry. I didn't understand it then but I trusted you as my spiritual parents. While going through this process of waiting, I know today that GOD was doing a great work on the inside of me. I had the call but I wasn't ready! Thank you for making me wait and not putting me out there before it was time.

In conclusion, I am confident that much of my success is a direct result of the law of honor. Mike Murdock said, "Your future is determined by those you choose to honor." With that in mind, I honor you Bishop & Co-Pastor McCarter with the dedication of my book, "Rivers of Life, a Collection of Life-changing Sermons & Homilies". Your labor is not in vain. This book is a demonstration of your ministry in action.

HONORABLE MENTIONS

Roman 12:10 ***(NIV) Love each other deeply. Honor others more than yourselves.***

To my mentor, Lady Leah Hill McNair – Words cannot express my gratitude and sincere appreciation for your endless sacrifices and determination to empower women in ministry. You are definitely an unsung hero. On behalf of all the women in ministry that you have inspired to be GREAT, I honor you!

Thank you for being a priceless gift to the kingdom of GOD. The body of Christ is altogether better because of you, Lady Leah. Your fingerprints have been left on the lives of many all across this world. Your labor has not been in vain. I am so blessed to have you as my mentor. I honor you!

To my Greater Cleveland Avenue Christian Church (GCACC) family, Thank you for your prayers, unfailing love and support in all that I do. I honor you!

To all of my family and friends, you have seen me through both the best of times and the worst of times. I appreciate having a safe place in you where I can be transparent without judgment. Your loyalty and commitment to assist me in making all of my dreams a reality have paid off! I honor you!

To the best, five-star marketing team in the world, B2L Graphic Design & Photography, you are indeed a blessing to me. God could not have given me a better group of anointed people who could supernaturally transform my "many" spontaneous ideas into works of art like you! Thanks for all you do. I honor you!

Last but not least, to my publisher, MACPUB, thanks for your patience and persistence to see this project come forth with excellence. I honor you!

DISCOVERING THE GOD IN ME...
THE RIVER OF LIFE!

Out of your belly shall flow rivers of living water... John 7:38

For many years, like the woman at the well found in the book of John, I found myself thirsty, going through the motions, going to draw water time after time to meet my needs, living life, yet still empty and dissatisfied. After having had an undeniable experience with GOD and having no clue that HE had invested a part of Himself on the inside of me, regardless of my past failures, I realized that He chose me and had a great plan for my life as evidenced by the words of Jer. 29:11, "I know the plans I have for you says God, plans of peace and not of evil to give you an expected end."

Like this woman at the well, I discovered my purpose, His power and the potential to do great things. It was at that "GOD moment" of discovery that I too dropped my water pots, the things in my life that I held on to seemingly satisfy my thirst. Why? I realized that there was a RIVER OF LIFE in my belly! John 7:38 A river that can and will change the lives of others. Like the woman at the well, for many years, I carried out the work of an evangelist, sharing my testimony, preaching, teaching and praying for others in homeless shelters, correctional institutions, hospitals, nursing homes, treatment centers and the like. Without a ministerial license, I saw the POWER of GOD transform lives through the Word of GOD!

Today, as I embark upon my eighth year in ministry as a licensed and ordained Elder, GOD has challenged me to put many of these life-changing words to print by writing this book of short sermons and homilies to empower and encourage YOU!

My prayer is that GOD will utilize the words found in this collection to flow like a river into every dry place in your life. May the person reading this book who many times invests in others seeds of faith and encouragement, find encouragement. May the wounded soul find hope and healing and most of all, may this be the beginning of the BEST days of your life!

1
THE NILE RIVER - "FAITH"

DROP THE CHARGES

LUKE 23: 34
34Then said Jesus, Father, forgive them; for they know not what they do.

The scene had been set. Jesus had been betrayed by one of his closest associates, Judas Iscariot. He had been stripped of his clothes and beaten viciously and brutally, to the point that he was unrecognizable! In my own imagination, I can hear him say, "Father, forgive them; for they know not what they do!" It is here that I would like to begin my argument with this text. What would make Jesus use his precious strength and energy to PRAY for these trifling, scandalous, treacherous and ungrateful individuals? They were the very ones who had betrayed Him and set Him up, causing this torture and pain in His life. Notice this wasn't a prayer of "Vengeance is mine. Kill them father! For, they have done me wrong." He said, "Father, forgive them; for they know not what they do."

The word forgive is defined as in some cases, to dismiss and/or drop the charges. In the court of law, there are times when the District Attorney, whose job it is to represent the victim and to ensure that justice is served, may get a bit frustrated, especially when a victim says things like DROP THE CHARGES! Forgive them; for they know not what they do. In the text, although witnesses were present and provided written statements found in the synoptic gospels, Matthew, Mark, and Luke, Jesus did not try to get even or fight so that justice might be served. He simply said, "Forgive them. Drop the charges!"

If you're going to be effective in the things of GOD, you have to understand the lesson that Jesus was teaching right here from the cross. It was the lesson of forgiveness. Below are some principles on the ways in which to walk in the power of forgiveness.

1. DON'T LET YOUR DILEMMA DROWN YOU!

Oftentimes, when we are faced with discomfort, betrayal and the like, we get so distracted by our dilemma to the point that we can no longer function and carry out our assignments. It appears to have overwhelmed us to the point that we're not physically able to fulfill our purpose. Jesus, unlike most of us, was in pain but He kept right on speaking into the lives of others while hanging on a cross. Don't you dare let your DILEMA drown you.

2. RECOGNIZE THAT THERE IS PURPOSE & POWER IN YOUR PAIN

Settle it in your heart. If you're going to reign with Him, at times you may have to suffer with Him. There will be seasons of betrayal, hurt and disappointments. Realize that you too are a partaker of Christ's suffering. Be confident that what you're going through has purpose and power. The Word of God says all of these things are going to work together for your good. The word all is the inclusion of everything and the exclusion of nothing! It all has purpose! When you understand that your pain has purpose and power, you, like Jesus, will understand how to respond rather than react to the dirt that is being done to you.

3. RESPOND, RATHER THAN REACT

This is not the time for you to react in the flesh, going off, acting all out of character when people do just what people do! Nowhere in the text do we see Jesus trying to hire a hit man. Nowhere in the text was He trying to defend the allegations. Nowhere in the text was He trying to track down a lie. Let's just be honest. There have been times when I wanted to get even. I was angry and I wanted revenge! I HAD TO LEARN how to DROP THE CHARGES!!! Realizing that what I was dealing with had purpose, I could not afford to go off and abort my destiny by reacting out of my flesh.

In our text, Judas Had a PLAN but in the midst of it all, GOD had a PURPOSE. I am so glad Jesus did not respond in the flesh, but rather He prayed, "Father, forgive them; for they know not what they do." When we respond in faith to our dilemmas, we too will be empowered to pray for our enemies.

Matt 5:44-45
44... Love your enemies, bless them that curse you, do good to them that hate you, and pray for them which despitefully use you, and persecute you;

In closing, perhaps you realize that the issues in your life have been holding you hostage. Find a way today to DROP THE CHARGES. Yes, it happened and it hurt! You may have wanted to get even, but choose to DROP THE CHARGES! Choose to release them and release yourself from the mental turmoil of the past! Father, Forgive them; for they know not what they do!

STEPPING OUT!

Mark 5: 25 -34

[25] And a certain woman, which had an issue of blood twelve years,[26] And had suffered many things of many physicians, and had spent all that she had, and was nothing bettered, but rather grew worse,[27] When she had heard of Jesus, came in the press behind, and touched his garment.[28] For she said, If I may touch but his clothes, I shall be whole.[29] And straightway the fountain of her blood was dried up; and she felt in her body that she was healed of that plague.[30] And Jesus, immediately knowing in himself that virtue had gone out of him, turned him about in the press, and said, Who touched my clothes?[31] And his disciples said unto him, Thou seest the multitude thronging thee, and sayest thou, Who touched me?[32] And he looked round about to see her that had done this thing.[33] But the woman fearing and trembling, knowing what was done in her, came and fell down before him, and told him all the truth.[34] And he said unto her, Daughter, thy faith hath made thee whole; go in peace, and be whole of thy plague.

There are times in our lives when we are faced with all kinds of challenges, disappointments, heartaches, etc. Although you have been praying and fasting and praising, it seems like what you're going through is not getting any better, but worse. You have asked the questions, "Lord why me? What am I to do now?" When you don't know what to do, I am confident that you can have rest, peace and joy in the presence of the Lord. I am reminded of the Word of God in Psalm 16:11 "In your presence there is fullness of joy."

I believe that perhaps this woman in our text was longing for a change in her life; longing for the opportunity to get into the presence of the Lord, in hopes that in some way her condition would get better. All that she had tried in her own strength had not worked. Perhaps, this woman had become discouraged. Maybe she had grown sick and tired of being sick and tired. Let's face it, for twelve (12) years she had been hemorrhaging blood, 4,380 days of a consistent flow without any relief! She had to be going through some physical changes and if that was not enough, she also had to have experienced some mental turmoil and depression from having become a social outcast. Can you imagine having friends and family one day and the next, everybody has abandoned you because of your condition?

After having heard about all the miracles that Jesus had performed, I believe she cried out and said, "I've been in this situation for twelve (12) years. When is it going to be my time? Somebody, anybody, Usher ME into the presence of the LORD!" Although she had been labeled unclean, she got up and did something about her situation. She took a risk in order to get into the presence of God, against the customs of that day to CHANGE her situation. I am confident that some things in your life are not going to change until you become willing to take the first step. Are you willing to step out of your comfort zone to go to a place you have never gone before; to experience that which you have never experienced?

This woman could have stayed bound by her situation. I am sure that after twelve years she had grown accustomed to the way her life was. However, somewhere on the inside of her, she maintained a dream; a vision for her life that things would not stay the same! DO what you have to do. Be willing to take the first step even if you have to do it alone! Opportunity is waiting on the other side of your fears and reservations. It is not the will of God to leave you in this same situation. He said, "I have come that you might have life and that you might have it more abundantly."

Step out in faith and watch GOD change things in your life. The text said it was her faith that made her whole. Your faith in GOD can do exceedingly and abundantly more than you could ever ask or think! Step out there on what seems to be nothing and receive the promises of stepping in faith!

SPEAK THE WORD

Matthew 8:23-27

"And when he was entered into a ship, his disciples followed him. And, behold, there arose a great tempest in the sea, insomuch that the ship was covered with the waves: but he was asleep. And his disciples came to him, and awoke him saying, Lord, save us: we perish. And he saith to them, Why are ye so fearful, O ye of little faith? Then he arose, and rebuked the winds and the sea; and there was a great calm. But the men marveled, saying, what manner of man is this, that even the winds and the sea obey him!"

In the society that we live in, we know a little something about storms. We have been face-to-face with all kinds of storms that have left the lives of many topsy-turvy. If we press rewind, in the early 90's, a storm hit in the form of a war called "desert storm." That storm claimed the lives of many young and old. In 2005, a storm by the name of Katrina took the lives of many people in the New Orleans, Louisiana area. If that was not enough, in 2010 all kinds of Tsunamis, earthquakes, and typhoons hit places like Japan and Haiti.

I am not a meteorologist but I realize that storms do not discriminate. Regardless of what side of town you live on, how much money you have in your bank account or perhaps the color of your skin, we all at some point in time have had to deal with a storm. While the storms may come in different forms, they all have somewhat the same results, destruction!

In our text, Jesus teaches a powerful lesson on how to handle the storms in your life.
Note that He did not operate in fear but used His authority and simply spoke to the storm. With that in mind, you too have to speak the Word. Jesus demonstrates the power of the spoken

word. When He operated in authority, it messed up everyone on the ship. They were like, "Wait a minute. What just happened? What manner of man is this? Even the winds and sea obey Him?" When you respond to the storms in your life the way in which Jesus responded, the wind and the sea are subject to the power speaking on the inside of you! You have to speak the Word! God has given you the keys to the kingdom that whatever YOU bind on earth will be bound in heaven and whatever YOU lose in earth will be loosed in heaven. So, what's stopping you from speaking the word?

The weapons of your warfare are not carnal but they are mighty through God to the pulling down of strongholds. It's time for you to speak the WORD! When you are going through a storm in your life, find a scripture. All you need is one. Find a scripture that supports what you believe God for. Once you find it, speak it out of your mouth every day, perhaps a couple of times a day until it becomes a part of your spirit. Speak the Word out loud so the devil can hear it! Not only that, when you speak, it ignites your faith. The bible says, "Faith cometh by hearing and hearing by the word of GOD." Speak the Word! You have to make it up in your mind to speak the Word no matter what! An unexpected storm may have hit your body. Speak the Word, "I shall not die but I shall live to declare the works of the Lord." Speak the Word, "He was wounded my transgression He was bruised for my iniquities and by His strips I am healed." Speak the Word, "Health and healing are in my house and no infirmity can live in my body." Speak the Word, He is the King of kings and the Lord of lords; He is Jehovah Rapha—my healer, who heals all matter of diseases. SPEAK THE WORD!

You may be in a financial storm. Speak the Word. Life and death are in the power of your tongue. The bible says that you can decree a thing and it shall be established. Don't wait for someone else to decree it. You begin to speak the Word and tell the devil, "I have never seen the righteous forsaken nor His seed having to beg for bread." Speak, "I shall lend and not borrow. I shall spend my days in pleasure and my years in prosperity." Speak the Word. "God shall supply all of my needs according to His riches in Glory." He will rebuke the devourer for my sake because I'm a tither and a giver! Speak the Word. He gives seed to the sower. He is making my way prosperous and I shall have good success.

If you simply speak the Word, the Word will speak for itself! His Word will not return to Him void but it shall accomplish the very thing that He sent it out to do. Never allow your mouth to speak defeat or doubt. The keys to your destiny are in your mouth. What are you speaking? If you are speaking anything that contradicts His Word and His purpose for your life, STOP IT!

As of this day, by the authority invested in me, in the name of the Father, the Son, and the Holy Ghost, I charge every one of you reading this to begin to speak the Word of God over your life and situation. Speak the Word with boldness and authority so much so that every time you speak, it bombards the gates of hell. I charge you this day to speak the Word in season and out of season. When you don't feel like it, speak the Word. When you are in pain, speak the Word. Speak the Word and let the Word do the work!

I'M IN PROTECTIVE CUSTODY

Psalm 91
He that dwelleth in the secret place of the most High shall abide under the shadow of the Almighty. I will say of the Lord, He is my refuge and my fortress: my God; in him will I trust. Surely he shall deliver thee from the snare of the fowler, and from the noisome pestilence. He shall cover thee with his feathers, and under his wings shalt thou trust: his truth shall be thy shield and buckler. Thou shalt not be afraid for the terror by night; nor for the arrow that flieth by day; Nor for the pestilence that walketh in darkness; nor for the destruction that wasteth at noonday. A thousand shall fall at thy side, and ten thousand at thy right hand; but it shall not come nigh thee. Only with thine eyes shalt thou behold and see the reward of the wicked. Because thou hast made the Lord, which is my refuge, even the most High, thy habitation; There shall no evil befall thee, neither shall any plague come nigh thy dwelling. For he shall give his angels charge over thee, to keep thee in all thy ways. They shall bear thee up in their hands, lest thou dash thy foot against a stone. Thou shalt tread upon the loin and adder: the young lion and the dragon shalt thou trample under feet. Because he hath set his love upon me, therefore will I deliver him: I will set him on high, because he hath known my name. He shall call upon me, and I will answer him: I will be with him in trouble; I will deliver him, and honour him. With long life will I satisfy him, and show him my salvation.

Many of you are saved, sanctified and filled with the Holy Ghost as it is evidenced by your speaking in tongues. However, with all of that said, there are still days that you feel like you have been victimized. What I mean by being victimized is that you have been abused by what we call life; everyday life and everyday struggles. You know life's ups and downs with all of the other spontaneous things that just seem to happen, which sometimes leave you saying, "Doggone. If it's not one thing, then it's another." It appears that the enemy has an all out attack against you. We know he does because his assignment is to kill, steal and destroy. He has made attempt after attempt to kill you, to kill your faith with fear, to kill your family with drama, and to kill your finances with debt and unexpected expenses. That's not all. He has even tried to steal your joy, to steal your peace of mind, and to steal your confidence in God.

Regardless of what your struggle has been, according to Psalms 91:1-11, you are in protective custody. The United States Constitution has a specialized program in place that provides protection and security for its witnesses. This program is carried out by US Marshalls, who are obligated to make sure no hurt, harm or danger comes upon either the individual or those in their immediate family. Stick with me. Did you know that your Heavenly Father has a protective custody program? When you made a decision to become a witness for the Lord, He became obligated to keep you in all of your ways. There is nothing in your life that is going on right now that He is not aware of. Be confident and stand on His Word! Don't take my word for it. Check out the terms and conditions of the protective custody order that has been released over your life found in Psalm 91. The program has been executed by God the Father and He has angels are on assignment to keep you, to protect that which concerns you. Have no fear, but FAITH! You are in protective custody. In this program, you have some additional rights found in Matt. 16:19 to bind and to lose. It's time to rise up and take a stand! Don't give up and don't give in. Cry if you must, feel all your feelings but when you're done dealing with the issues, be confident that GOD is still in control, because YOU ARE IN PROTECTIVE CUSTODY!

As a witness for the Lord, you have rights. You have a right to rebuke the devil! Stop allowing him to stalk and harass you with all kinds of foolishness. You may have done some things in your past that you are not proud of but so what! The truth of the matter is that we have all done some stuff that we are not proud of. II Corinthians 5:17 says "Therefore if any man be in Christ, he is a new creature: old things are passed away; behold, all things are become new." The past is the past! Rebuke the devil and move on. You are in Protective Custody. You also have the right to rest according to Psalms 91:11 "God has given His angels charge over you to keep you in all of your ways." Now, that is some good news to me! That lets me know that He is omnipresent and omnipotent. So, even if you are stuck in a rut or your body is racked with pain, you can still sleep in peace. Psalms 46:1 tells us that He is a very present help in the time of trouble. So, there is no use in staying up all night! You might as well rest. Sleep on knowing that you are in protective custody.

Last but not least, you have the right to receive the promises of God! How can I be sure? Even when you are going through something, the Word assures you that the promises of God in Him are still yes and amen. The promises of God are not dependent upon the economy, man or whether or not they like you. When you are in protective custody, He is in control of everything in the heavens and the earth. So, you can rest and then you can receive the promise that some way, somehow, God is going to get the promise to you. A promise is still a promise!

I pray that this has given you hope that everything is going to work together for your good. You may have stayed up all night crying and worrying yourself sick but let the Word remind you that "weeping may endure for a night but joy cometh in the morning." You have to know when sickness hits your body and you feel like you are about to die that He was wounded for your transgressions,

He was bruised for your iniquities, and by His strips you are healed. Not only that, but you shall live and not die and declare the works of the Lord.

I must offer a disclaimer of truth. If you don't know Jesus as your personal Savoir, then you are not in protective custody. Protective custody is a benefit of your relationship with Jesus Christ. God doesn't require you to be perfect but He requires effort. So, if you want to tap into this thing called protective custody, get to know Him ASAP! You have a life to live and a God to glorify. So, being under protective custody should mean more to you than anything else. In closing, you have a right to live the life that Jesus died for you to have. Live it in PROTECTIVE CUSTODY!

USHER ME INTO THE PRESENCE OF THE LORD

Psalm 16: 11
"You will show me the path of life, In Your presence is fullness of joy; At Your right hand are pleasures forevermore."

As Christians, we are not exempt from suffering but we can find strength, joy and peace in the presence of the LORD. The bible is filled with people who came face-to-face with stressful situations that could have gotten the best of them. However, after having an encounter with GOD, suddenly everything changed. I want to encourage you on today that GOD sees all. He knows all and He has not forgotten about you. The truth is there ain't no mountain high enough, there ain't no valley low enough, there ain't even a river wide enough to keep the presence of GOD from you. Call upon Him in your time of distress according to Jer 33:3 and He will answer you and show you great and mighty things. In addition to prayer, worship is another key to get into His presence. God has promised that as we draw near to Him, He will draw near to us and we will experience His presence. On today, even if there is fear in your heart and tears in your eyes, find a way to pray and muster up praise. Worship the Lord your God for who He is, what He has done in times past and what He is capable of doing right now!

He is a very present help in the time of a storm. He is the kind of man that will never leave you nor forsake you. The next time you find yourself in what appears to be a lose-lose situation, tap into His presence. In his presence, there is fullness of joy. With the presence and the power of GOD with you, all you do is WIN-WIN!

EXPECTING A RIDICULOUS BLESSING

Luke 1: 30-32
"And the angel said unto her, Fear not, Mary: for thou hast found favour with God. And, behold, thou shalt conceive in thy womb, and bring forth a son, and shalt call his name Jesus. He shall be great, and shall be called the Son of the Highest:"

The word expecting is defined as to look forward to, anticipate, or being pregnant in the progressive tense. With that in mind, Mary, the mother of Jesus, was expecting what some would call a Ridiculous Blessing. After having received the Word from the Lord and having to deal with the possible rejection of her fiancé Joseph, there had to be some emotional conflicts that she had to overcome in order to obtain the blessing! The truth of the matter is when we are waiting on the manifestation of a promise, we all get a little frustrated. When in the natural it doesn't look like anything is happening, it will make you feel like your waiting is a waste of time. You may feel like you are stuck living between the Prophecy and the Promise because what you are experiencing is not what you have been expecting from GOD! It can be rather frustrating living like Hannah, a woman of a sorrowful spirit. It seems like the more you pray and believe God for your breakthrough, it seems to keep happening for everybody else. You've cried, you've prayed, you've fasted but you're still expecting. We can find hope today in Isaiah 40:31 "But they that wait upon the Lord shall renew their strength; they shall mount up with wings as eagles; they shall run, and not be weary, and they shall walk, and not faint."

When it comes to waiting on GOD, we have to be reminded that our thoughts are not God's thoughts and our ways are not His ways. Could it be that our waiting is preparing us for something great? We have got to learn how to trust the process and begin to view the season of waiting as an opportunity to prepare, position and push ourselves. Mary teaches us how to do these three things in the text. Preparation - When a woman is expecting a baby, at first there are no significant physical changes. However, she begins to make plans for the name, the bed, the room, etc. When it comes to the things of God, you must begin making preparation. During this preparation phase, you may experience a few emotional roller coasters, but put first things first according to Psalm 46:10 "Be still and know that I am God." It is of utmost importance that you get your emotions in CHECK! So many times, we make situations more than they are due to our own anxiety. CALM DOWN! God has your life under control. He knows how to handle even the most seemingly complex situations with ease.

Secondly, in this phase of preparation you have to stand in faith, no matter what. Romans 1:17 -"The just shall live by faith." Nowhere in the text do you see Mary running around trying to justify what has been spoken to her. She evidently made a decision to stand in faith and believe GOD. Never try to explain or get people to understand the promises that God made you! They won't be convinced, and half the time, even if they know the truth, they won't celebrate your success and promise anyway. Some people will just have to see it to believe it. Wait and let them see you healed, blessed, etc. Don't waste your time and energy explaining and justifying anything else. It is what it is. GOD said it and that settles it. Prepare yourself for your promise, but also prepare for the persecution. You don't owe anyone an explanation about what God has done, is doing and shall do in you and through you for His glory!

After having spent some time in preparation for the promise you have been expecting, you must position yourself around others that will celebrate the GOD on the inside of you. In the text, Mary visited Elizabeth and the baby (promise) that she was waiting for began to leap. I see something here. If you're going to be successful in carrying this baby full term, it is important that you surround yourself with the right people. The wrong kind of exposure can contaminate that which is on the inside of you. You must guard your heart from any form of fear, doubt and unbelief. Matthew 16:19 "And I will give unto thee the keys to the Kingdom of Heaven: and whatsoever thou shalt bind on earth shall be bound in heaven: and whatsoever thou shalt loose on earth shall be loosed in heaven." You have the right to position yourself to receive the promises of GOD by conducting spiritual warfare when necessary. Stand firm, being confident that the kingdom of heaven suffers violence, but the violent take it by force. Put on the whole armor of GOD that you may be able to stand against the wiles of the devil! For the weapons of our warfare are not carnal but mighty through GOD to the pulling down of strong holds. We wrestle not against flesh and blood, but principalities, spiritual wickedness in high places! Position yourself as a warrior and fight for the manifestation of that which you have been carrying in your heart. The vision shall come to past. Prepare, position yourself and finally, if you're going to receive your ridiculous blessings (things that make absolutely no sense and are completely mind-blowing) in this season, you have to push.

In this season of your life, I need to remind you that you have come too far to turn back now. Keep pushing! Don't you dare give up and throw in the towel. Keep pushing. Find a way to push pass what you're feeling. Focus on Roman 8, that all of these things are going to work for your good, because the suffering of this present time is not worthy to be compared with the glory that shall be revealed. Keep pushing!!! Pray Until Something Happens! Praise Until Something Happens! Whatever you do, don't you quit! Your persistence will pay off!

What would have happened if Mary would have given up? None of us would have the gift of eternal life. Like Mary, remind yourself that you have found favor with GOD and you shall bring forth every promise that has been made to you by GOD! Your expectations are not in vain. You have a right to expect big things from GOD. Some people have to see it to believe it. I am confident that you have to BELIEVE it in order to see it! Expect the ridiculous from GOD! He can and He will do exceedingly and abundantly above all that you may ask or think!

THERE IS A MIRACLE IN YOUR MOUTH

Matthew 17: 27
"Notwithstanding, lest we should offend them, go thou to the sea, and cast an hook, and take up the fish that first cometh up; and when thou hast opened his mouth, thou shalt find a piece of money: that take, and give unto them for me and thee."

Many years ago, there was a famous TV Show that came on every Sunday Morning by the name of Gospel Expo. On that show, I can remember hearing a song, "I'm looking for a miracle... I expect the impossible." When you begin to think about the state of the economy and the many struggles we face in our everyday lives, We ALL have been in need of a Miracle. Have you ever had the feeling of frustration knowing that you were not where you knew you should be in life or that you were not getting everything you were supposed to get out of life? You had a feeling that life was full of possibilities, but somehow you could never figure out how to tap into them. Has there ever been a time when it seemed like there was a black cloud over you? Everywhere you turned, there was some type of drama or disappointment, to the point that it had you questioning "What is wrong with me?" When is it going to be my time?" You are not alone. Many people have come to believe that life is a mystery that cannot be solved. They think that success and prosperity are destined for everyone except them. They feel powerless and victimized as the events of their lives spiral out of control.

Perhaps, like the fish in our text, there is the miracle that you have been waiting for and it's in our mouth. A miracle is any amazing or wonderful occurrence; a marvelous event manifesting a supernatural act of God.; an intervention by God in the universe; a manifestation of perfection; an event in the natural world, but out of its established order, possible only by the intervention of divine power; an event that cannot be explained by the known laws of nature and is therefore, attributed to a supernatural or divine power.

In other words, a miracle is something so great that it must be God. It cannot be explained and or proved by science. It's a miracle. It cannot be bought! You receive the miracles in your life by faith. If you do a study of Jesus and the various miracles He performed, you will note that the miracle was received according to the person's faith. Here is the point of the matter. There is a miracle in your mouth! You have what it takes to change your life and the world on the inside of you. In Genesis, God proved to us the miracles that were in His mouth when he said something and it was manifested.

Do you have the faith to speak and suddenly your situation changes? The miracle you are looking for is in your mouth. Speak what the Word says concerning your life and your individual situations. The bible says that "death and life is in the power of your own tongue." You have a right to speak those things that be not as though they were. Speak confidently that whatsoever you desire when you pray believe that you receive and you shall have them. There is a miracle in your mouth! If you can see it, believe it, because you can achieve it. The miracles are locked up in your mouth. Say it, say it, say it and you can have it!

2

THE RIVER OF SIHON ~ "POWER & AUTHORITY"

I GOT THE POWER

Acts 1:8
"But ye shall receive power, after that the Holy Ghost is come upon you: and ye shall be witnesses unto me both in Jerusalem, and in all Judaea, and in Samaria, and unto the uttermost part of the earth."

In the society in which we live, lots of people live in fear due to a number of different things like crime, sickness and especially the state of the economy, just to name a few. When they look at natural things like the prices of gas and food, they tend to fear and doubt and some get so overwhelmed with anxiety and stress that they become hopeless and helpless. For many people they have put their hope and faith in the stock market, believing that there is power in the almighty dollar bill. Some tend to define their lives by the amount of money they have in the bank, the car they drive and/or the labels on their clothes. For some reason, these things make them feel powerful. However, the moment they get laid off or receive an unexpected report, they lose all that power. This is like some church folk I know who have a form of Godliness but deny the power. They look the part but there is a missing ingredient; the presence and the power of the Holy Ghost. Allow me to introduce you to just a few of His many characteristics.

According to John 14:26, "But the comforter, which is the holy ghost, whom the father will send in my name, he shall teach you all things, and bring all things to your remembrance, whatsoever I have said unto you." He is known to many as a Teacher. The purpose of the Holy Spirit in your life is to teach you His truths and help you to accomplish the things God has called you to do. There is nothing hidden that will not be revealed! The Power Source will teach you and show you all things and make known to you the mysteries of the gospel. This is how you have access to information and you know things that you have no proof of! The Holy Ghost!

John 14:16-17 states "And I will pray the Father and He shall give you another comforter, that he may abide with you forever; 17 even the spirit of truth; whom the world cannot receive, because it seeth him not, neither knoweth him: but ye know him; for he dwelleth with you, and shall be in you." Not only is the Holy Spirit a teacher, He is a comforter. He is the One that promises never to leave you or forsake you. The Holy Spirit is the very presence of God, a very present help in the time of trouble. He has the ability to embrace you, console you and provide protection and guidance as He leads you into all truth. He assists you in carrying out the plan of God for your life so that you might be about your Father's business.

Finally, He is a protector. He will keep you out of hell. Acts 2:26-28, "Therefore, did my heart rejoice, and my tongue was glad; moreover also my flesh shall rest in hope: 27 because thou wilt not leave my soul in hell, neither wilt thou suffer thine holy one to see corruption. 28 thou hast made known to me the ways of life; thou shalt make me full of joy with thy countenance." This gives me hope that He loved me so much that He would not allow my soul to remain in hell! Now, if that's not enough to make you want to shout and dance, then I don't know what will. When I just think about how He could have allowed me to wake up in hell with no opportunity to return. I don't know about you, but I haven't been saved all of my life. He covered me! I have done some things in my day but I thank God for the Holy Ghost that has kept me! He kept me from falling back into an old life of sin. He kept me from the hand of the enemy.

Allow me to testify about the power, protection and purpose of the Holy Ghost in my own life. Some years ago, I recall having come face-to-face with what the devil thought would be my demise. But God! I am talking about the power of the Holy Ghost! As I stood there, face-to-face with the enemy, with a gun pointed to my head, hearing but not listening to the voices of others around me, who where crying out in fear, "Stop! Stop! Oh my God! He is going to kill her! No! No!" In faith, not fear I stood! I stood in the power of the Holy Ghost! Not looking to the left or to the right, I continued to stand eyeball to eyeball with the enemy. As he cocked the gun back, promising that he would kill me, I decreed and declared, "You just might shoot me, but you will not kill me! The Word of the Lord says no weapon formed against me shall prosper!" At that moment, it seemed as though my statement of faith added fuel to the fire. In a rage, he then pulled the trigger and the gun got jammed! The only reason I was able to walk out of that situation was the power of the Holy Ghost.

I am not telling you what I read. I am telling you what I know from personal experiences. There are benefits to having the power of the Holy Ghost! I've got the power and so do you! The Holy Ghost is that source of power needed to endure everyday issues. In addition, it empowers you with the necessary tools to engage in spiritual warfare. We know Him (Holy Spirit) to be the renewing, rejuvenating power of God on the inside of us. You have the power to tread on serpents and scorpions and the power to bind and loose! The presence of this power in you is the key to the kingdom. You are packing power! Don't let the devil punk you out of the promises of God! You've got the power of the Holy Ghost!

This power doesn't have anything to do with your bank account. The awesome thing about it is that this power can not be bought. You simply have to receive it by faith! You've got the power. So, use it for the glory of God! When Peter, full of power, stood up to preach, 3,000 folks were saved. God is no respecter of persons. You've got the power. Work it! This power is the burden-removing, yoke-destroying power of God inside of you! You've got the power!

IT'S MINE & I WANT IT BACK!

Luke 15:8
"Either what woman having ten pieces of silver, if she lose one piece, doth not light a candle, and sweep the house, and seek diligently till she find it?"

I wonder if there is anybody out there who has ever lost anything. If you are anything like me, you can't stand to lose anything. I will tear up a house looking for something I have misplaced. Why, you might ASK? Because it's mine and I want it back! I must admit, there are some things in my life that I have lost and Lord knows, I don't want them back! It cost me too much; too much time, too much energy, too much heartache and too many headaches! The truth be told, after all the hell I've been through, I ought to be thanking GOD, saying, "FREE at LAST. FREE at LAST. Thank GOD almighty. I'm FREE at LAST!"

In our text, there is a woman, who has lost something of *significant value!* Her SILVER coin was equivalent to a day's wages and was of great value. Do you have anything in your life that is so priceless that you cannot live without? As for me, I refuse to live without my relationship with GOD! At times, life can come at you so fast, you feel like what you've lost is not worth fighting for. Perhaps you're hopeless, entangled in life's ups and downs, disappointments and the enemy's web of deception and sin. It is at this point that you realize you have lost your passion for life and ministry. You have lost your joy, lost your faith and lost your zeal for the things of GOD!

This woman in our text has experienced a loss. However, in noticing her strategy, it is clear that she had it, she lost it but she got it back! Perhaps these principles will assist you in recovering all that has been lost in your life. Luke 15:8 "What woman having ten pieces of silver, if she lose one piece, doth not light a candle, and sweep the house, and seek diligently till she find it?"

1. COME OUT OF DARKNESS
The first thing this woman did was to make a decision to COME OUT OF DARKNESS! She lit a candle that eliminated the darkness in her life. Darkness is defined as the lack of knowledge; ignorance; to be uninformed; wickedness or evil; and absence or deficiency of light. In other words, darkness is anything that blocks you from the will of GOD and hinders your ability to see things as they really are. Sin is often the root of the darkness in our lives. God made a perfect world but then another element, sin, entered and the whole earth became polluted with darkness.

GOD is requiring us to COME out of DARKNESS! "You are a chosen generation, a royal priesthood, a holy nation, a peculiar people that ye should shew forth the praises of him who hath called you out of darkness into his marvelous light."

2. CLEAN HOUSE – PUT IN THE WORK!
The second thing the woman did in her process of recovery was to sweep the house. Once she turned on the light, she had to do something with the things that perhaps she had been falling over in the dark. Maybe you too need to make a decision to sweep your spiritual house clean. The good news is that according to I John 1:9, "If we confess our sins, He is faithful and just to forgive us our sins and to cleanse us from all unrighteousness." Keep in mind that whatever it takes for you to get clean, (healed, delivered and set free) it's going to take that and more to stay clean.

Matthew 12:43-45
43 When the unclean spirit is gone out of a man, he walketh through dry places, seeking rest, and findeth none. 44 Then he saith, I will return into my house from whence I came out; and

when he is come, he findeth it empty, swept, and garnished.[45] *Then goeth he, and taketh with himself seven other spirits more wicked than himself, and they enter in and dwell there: and the last state of that man is worse than the first. Even so shall it be also unto this wicked generation.*

With that in mind, it is of the utmost importance that you establish and maintain your spiritual house at all times. Come out of darkness and clean house!

3.   DON'T QUIT – DILIGENTLY SEEK
Joel 2:25 "And I will restore to you the years that the locust, the cankerworm, and the caterpillar, and the palmerworm had eaten." You have to hold on to the Word of GOD, no matter what and continue to seek Him. At times, life will zap all of your strength to the point that you feel like your choice to come out of darkness and clean house is not working! Be confident today that your labor is not in vain!

In the text, this woman diligently sought after the coin she lost. Although she could have grown weary on the journey, she did not quit. Today, you may feel like you are at the end of your rope. Let me encourage you to hold on! You've got a right to live the life JESUS died for you to have! DON'T QUIT! Just as this woman's lost coin was restored, I am confident that if you work these principles, GOD will restore everything in your life!

THE INTERRUPTION OF EVERYTHING

2 Kings 4:15-20

15 And he said, Call her. And when he had called her, she stood in the door. 16 And he said, About this season, according to the time of life, thou shalt embrace a son. And she said, Nay, my lord, thou man of God, do not lie unto thine handmaid. 17 And the woman conceived, and bare a son at that season that Elisha had said unto her, according to the time of life. 18 And when the child was grown, it fell on a day, that he went out to his father to the reapers. 19 And he said unto his father, My head, my head. And he said to a lad, Carry him to his mother. 20 And when he had taken him, and brought him to his mother, he sat on her knees till noon, and then died.

In 2005, the renowned author, Terry McMillan wrote another best-selling book, entitled "The Interruption of Everything." In the novel, Marilyn, the main character found herself in the midst of a mid-life crisis. She also found herself overwhelmed with some unexpected events that seemingly interrupted all that she had worked for; her family, her marriage – EVERYTHING! We all have had those unexpected events; a crisis that seemed to knock all of the air out of us. Never in a million years would you ever have seen the situation coming. Now, all that you have been planning and believing God for has been interrupted.

The term interruption is defined as to break the continuity or uniformity of something; to hinder or to stop the action or discourse of someone. On the other hand, crisis means a condition of instability or danger, as in social, economic, political, or international affairs leading to a decisive change; a dramatic, emotional or circumstantial upheaval in a person's life. It is an emotional and stressful event that sometimes forces you to change even when you don't want to change. In Chinese, the word crisis is composed of two distinct characters. One represents danger and the other represents opportunity. I recently heard someone say that a crisis is a divine announcement that something great is about to come!

In II Kings 4:15-20, we find a woman who although she loved the Lord and was minding her own business, she too faced an interruption of everything. However, this Shunammite woman can teach us a thing or two about how to handle a crisis! One particular day, while working in the field with his father, this woman's son had a crisis. It seemed like the very life had left his body. This woman could have become emotional. Her response to the situation could have been somewhat like that of an egg under pressure, and just cracked up. She could have lost her mind and ended up in the psyche ward not knowing what day it was, but she did not!

This Shunammite woman could have responded like an apple or a piece of fruit. Unlike the egg, the fruit has a little more substance to it. The thing about responding to things like a piece of fruit is that the right amount of pressure will tear your skin or open you up to the enemy. You look like you have the victory! You are all shined up looking like you can handle the crisis but every now and then, your stuff begins to ooze out of that small tear, attracting gnats and little flies. They tend to stick around you long enough to contaminate your faith, long enough to destroy you, then they move on to the next piece of fruit. Then, there are those of us, who like the Shunammite woman, tend to respond to situations like that of a tennis ball. The tennis ball has some tough skin. No matter how much pressure is on, it never loses its shape. Tennis ball people say I know how to take a licking and keep on ticking. Tennis ball people seem to find a way to bounce back, no matter what! This woman made a decision to bounce back from this crisis. Allow me to give you these six principles on how to handle the interruptions in your life as outlined in the text.

1. FIRST THINGS FIRST!

When the crisis happened, she took the boy back to the place where Elisha had made the promise! Matthew 6:33 says "But seek ye FIRST the kingdom of God, and his righteousness; and all these things shall be added unto you." The Word says in all of your ways acknowledge HIM and He will direct you path. Do not call everyone in town, asking their opinion of the matter. You have to learn how to put first things first!

2. SHUT THE DOOR!

When you find yourself in a crisis, you cannot afford to have people around you that don't believe like you believe. You have to learn how to shut the door to block out the haters, doubters and unbelievers! If they can't see what you see, if they can't believe like you believe, then you have to simply shut the door!

3. STAYED FOCUSED!

When the crisis happened, she didn't flip out. She had her mind made up that she was going to see something happen. She was focused! Nowhere in the text do we see where she stopped at her mama's house to let her mama look at the boy. Nowhere in the text do we see where she was calling girlfriends to get their opinion on the matter. She maintained laser focus. Like a horse, I believe she kept her face like flint, not moved to the left or the right. We have to establish and maintain our focus. Stop allowing the tactics of the enemy to get you off focus.

4. MAINTAIN A POSITIVE CONFESSION OF FAITH!

In the text, when the Shunammite woman arrived on the scene looking for the man of God, certain people started asking questions. Is everything alright? Is your husband alright? Is your son alright? However, she had a confession of faith, "All is well!" You have to have a positive confession of faith. I don't care how hard the crisis is in your life. You still have to confess what the Word says about you! The woman said, "All is well!"

5. BE BOLD AND COURAGEOUS!

The Word tells us that we can come boldly before the throne of grace and there, we can find mercy. So, even when we are frustrated, God can handle us saying, "What's up God? I'm a little ticked off about this because your Word promised me some things and what I am experiencing is not what I have been expecting. This is not what your Word says I can have!" God can handle you talking to Him like that. When the Shunammite woman got to Elisha she said, "Did I ask you for a son? Didn't I tell you not to lie to me!" She was bold! Elisha was like, "What's going on?" She responded, 'This son of mine of whom I didn't ask you for is laying in the room that we built for you and he looks like he is about to die. You need to do something!" Elisha was like, "Ok; calm down. I will send my assistant with my rod to lay on him." She said, "Oh no! I'm not leaving here without you! If you don't do it then it won't be done!" I wonder what would happen if you got that bold with God. Remind Him of what His word says concerning you. When you dare to be bold and courageous, God has to show up and change your situation!

6. TAKE AUTHORITY!

The bible says that the woman and Elisha got back to her house and they begin to take authority. The Word tells us that the kingdom of heaven suffereth violence and the violent have to take it by force. When stuff in your life is chaotic and there is an upheaval, it is time to take authority. We know that the weapon of our warfare is not carnal but mighty through God to the pulling down of strongholds. Moreover, we wrestle not with flesh and blood but against spiritual wickedness in high places. You have been equipped to bind the strongman! As believers, we cannot be possessed by the devil but we can be oppressed by the enemy! His imps and demons are on assignment to interrupt the plans of God for your life. You have to take authority over your atmosphere and your sphere of influence. Put the enemy in his proper place. Don't allow the devil to dominate your life when you have power and authority! Greater is He that is in you, then he who is in the world! You have to take authority! That is what Elisha and the woman of God did. The boy was laying there lifeless but they took authority. When they entered the room, they performed C.P.R. Not the kind of CPR that we think of in the natural. C – They closed the door! P – They began to Pray! R – The Resurrection took place! I wonder what would happen in your life if you made it up in your mind to take authority!

I would like to close with a quote from Mercedes Miller, **"EVERYTHING THAT YOU HAVE IS EVERYTHING THAT YOU NEED TO GET EVERYTHING THAT YOU WANT."** Don't allow the interruptions in your life to stop you from becoming and doing all that God has predestined for your life. God has equipped you with everything you need to be victorious in all things. God can and will interrupt the devil's plan!

I SEE YOU... DON'T QUIT!

Ezekiel 16:6
"And when I passed by thee, and saw thee polluted in thine own blood, I said unto thee when thou wast in thy blood, Live; yea, I said unto thee when thou wast in thy blood Live."

In our text, we find a woman in a struggle. I'm not sure what type of struggle she was in. However, the scripture said that she was struggling in her own blood. Have you ever found yourself in a struggle? Not just any struggle, but an issue you couldn't tell anybody about. So, you just kept it to yourself and hoped no one would notice that you were in a struggle. The truth of the matter is we don't always know who we can trust with our struggles. The fear of being judged or labeled will at times cause you to hold things in, to the point that it begins to hold you hostage. On the flip side, when your struggles are so obvious, some people tend to just walk on by and overlook you, knowing you're having a hard time.

The good news is whatever your struggle, the same GOD that saw this woman in our text, has seen you struggling day after day. He has seen you struggling to make ends meet. He has seen you struggling to keep a smile on your face when you really wanted to break down and scream! He has seen your tears and the nights you've walked the floor overwhelmed with sorrow and grief. Be encouraged on today. Like this struggling woman in the text, He see's you and is speaking life to your situation. Look at the text. The LORD spoke one Word and this woman's days of struggle were over! That one Word was LIVE. Yes, you may be in your own little quiet storm but don't you quit! LIVE! What's coming is better than what has been. Live through the struggle. For your sake, don't you dare give up before the miracle happens. God see's you in your struggle. YOU SHALL LIVE!

WALKING IN THE POWER OF NOW!

Isa. 43:18-19
Remember ye not the former things, neither consider the things of old. Behold, I will do a new thing; now it shall spring forth; shall ye not know it? I will even make a way in the wilderness, and rivers in the desert.

In reflecting and preparing for this message, I kept hearing the words of this popular song in my spirit. I know most of you been saved all your lives and your virgin ears may have never heard it, but for the purpose of this message, allow me to expose you for just a moment. It was performed by the R&B duo McFadden & Whitehead. The lyrics go a little something like this, "There've been so many things that have held us down, but now it looks like things are finally coming around. I know we've got a long, long way to go, and where we'll end up, I don't know. But, we won't let nothing hold us back, we gonna get ourselves together, we gonna polish up our act, yeah. If you've ever been held down before, I know that you refuse to be held down any more, yeah. Don't you let nothing stand in your way. I want you to listen to every word I say, every word I say. Ain't no stopping' us now. We're on the move!"

Will you be honest with me on today and admit, I've been through a lot of things but I have made it up in my mind that I am not going to let anything hold me back another day! I'm ready to walk in the power of now! In our text, the author offers a unique formula for those who are determined to walk in the power of now. Isaiah said, "Remember ye not the former things, neither consider the things of old. Behold, I will do a new thing; now it shall spring forth; shall ye not know it? I will even make a way in the wilderness, and rivers in the desert."

If you are going to walk in the power of my now, you are going to have to let the past be the past. The text instructs us to remember it no more. Oftentimes, we get so stuck living in yesterday that we fail to experience the gift of today. Living in the past with all of the would have's, could have's should have's is nothing more than a tool the enemy uses to keep you focused on the guilt, shame and condemnation. We all have been there at some point and time where we find ourselves performing spiritual CPR, breathing life into dead situations. On today, I want to encourage you to let the dead bury the dead. Make the decision to move on.

I am reminded of a woman in II Samuel by the name of Rizpa who missed out on the entire season of harvest grieving over her dead situations. Now, by no means am I downplaying the grieving process but what I am saying is that at some point, you have to get unstuck and know when it's time to move on. In the process of grieving, you eventually are encouraged to gain some level of acceptance of the facts in order to move on with life. Some have been carrying the hurt, disappointments and guilt for years, unable to shake it. Perhaps this is why the bible speaks about forgetting those things which are behind you and pressing on towards the mark of the prize of the high calling. It's over. It happened but don't spend anymore of your precious time and energy crying over spilled milk, trying to undo and/or redo things. The bible tells us not to even consider the things of old.

After letting go of the past, you must embrace the fact that God desires to do a new thing. Our comfort zone can rob us of our destiny and the promises of God that He has in store for us right now. Webster defines the word now as at the present time or moment; without further delay; immediately; at once. With that in mind it is of utmost importance that we seize the moment and not allow ourselves to become stuck in yesterday's failures and past mistakes. Establish and maintain the ability to live in the moment and be present to receive all that has been ordained for your life.

Indeed, it is your time and it is your turn to walk in the power of now. When thinking about this being your time and your season for your breakthrough, allow me to teach you for just a moment. There is a difference in time. Chronos refers to chronological or sequential time. There are 24 hours in a day. The first Greek term is chronos, meaning time on the move, time as before and after, time as the future passing through the present and so becoming the past. From this Greek word chronos, we derive such English terms as chronic, chronicle, and chronology. Thus, we call an illness chronic if it lasts a long time. A chronicle is an account of events through a sequence of time. Chronology is the itemized, studied measurement of time.

Kairos is an ancient Greek word meaning now, the right or opportune moment (the supreme moment) or a moment of indeterminate time in which something special happens. In the New Testament, kairos means "the appointed time in the purpose of God"; the time when God acts (e.g. Mark 1.15, The kairos is fulfilled). It differs from the more usual word for time which is chronos (kronos). Kairos cannot be measured because it is always in the now. A now is obviously invisible. An instant is too brief to account for. By the time you stop to measure a now, it has already gone. Furthermore, if now cannot be measured, it also can not be counted.

Stop worrying about what time it is or how old you are. It's time for you to operate in the kairos, your God moments - The now! You cannot afford to miss out on the move of GOD. The set time is NOW! Your past can't hold you hostage or dictate your future unless you allow it. The blood of Jesus paid the penalty for all of our sins. Today is your day to walk out of the shadows of your past and walk into the power of your present, the NOW!

FACE-OFF!
DEALING WITH THE REAL ME!

John 4:16-18
"Jesus said to her, Go, call your husband, and come here." 7 The woman answered and said, "I have no husband." Jesus said to her, "You have well said, 'I have no husband,' 18 for you have had five husbands, and the one whom you now have is not your husband; in that you spoke truly."

Many of us were raised in households where you often heard things like, "What happens in this house stays in this house." Such statements had somewhat of a valid purpose. However, for many, it taught us how to mask our feelings and emotions. Our culture has taught us how to go through the motions, put on the face as if everything is ok. We know how to put on the face. "Praise the Lord! Me, I am too blessed to be stressed, too anointed to be disappointed, Fire baptized in Jesus' name and I am still running for my life!" The truth behind the mask is that there is still some hurt, some pain, a sense of emptiness, rejection, abandonment and low self-esteem. To look at you, nobody would know you are recovering from mental turmoil like domestic violence, PTSD, or flashbacks from the abuse that happened to you as a child. Nobody knows the recurring nightmares that are seemingly killing you softly because you were told, "You better not tell anybody or else!"

We see the glory but we really don't know your story. We don't know about the harsh words that have been spoken over you like, You ain't nothing but a _____. You are going to be just you're your _____. You will never amount to anything. You are too fat, too skinny, too black and the list goes on and on. The verbal abuse and the physical, mental and emotional baggage have weighed you down long enough. Let's take a moment and take the face off and deal with the real issues. All of that baggage you have been hiding behind has robbed you spiritually, raped you mentally, and forever left you pregnant with twins named something and nothing! The good news is, the Word of God tells us that He has come to set the captives free! I decree and declare on today by the power of God that whom the son has made free is free indeed! Take off the face and let's keep it real!

I'm sure the woman in our text had her days of wearing a mask to cover up the pain, the guilt, the harsh words and opinions of others. However, on this particular day, she had an encounter with God that changed her life forever. Her purpose at the well was to simply draw water to quench her physical thirst and satisfy the needs of her household. However, while she was there, she had an encounter with God and she could no longer wear the mask as if everything was ok. He asked her a question and she took off the mask and began to deal with the real issues. It no longer mattered what she had been hiding behind.

In this text, I noticed that this woman did a few things to really get free from the image she had. First of all, she had to tell the truth, in verses 16 & 17, this woman got honest about herself and her situation. Paula White said it many years ago, "You can't conqueror what you won't confront!" Today is the day to tell the truth. That mask you've been hiding behind has served its purpose. It has protected you but today is the day to take off the mask! You've been in denial long enough. I John 1:9, "If you confess your sins, he is faithful and just to forgive you of your sins and cleanse you of all unrighteousness!" John 8:32, "and ye shall know the truth, and the truth shall make you free."

The next thing I noticed in this text is that she faced her fears and dropped her water pots. Are you willing to drop everything and everybody that is hindering you from God's best? Look at verse 28. Suddenly, she dropped her water pots (the ways and means of doing things just to survive) and went running through the city saying come see a man! I can only imagine that they thought this woman was crazy. Like her, some are going to think you are crazy for dropping the baggage in your life but so what! Let them think whatever they want. Drop it. There are some other people waiting for you to get free. Drop these water pots! Drop the mask you have been hiding behind and get healed and made completely whole so you can help someone else.

Finally, like the woman in our text, you have a right to live the life Jesus died for you to have. Perhaps, that is why He was so determined to wait for her at the well; to give her an opportunity to take off the mask and tell the truth about her struggle. He came so that we might have life and have it more abundantly. You gain that abundant life when you ask for forgiveness, forgive yourself and others! When you refuse to do this and continue to wear the "tough guy" mask like everything is ok and nothing matters, then you find yourself constantly re-living past events over and over again. You remain stuck in the past, denying yourself what is needed to grow and become all that you were born to be.

Forgiveness is said to be the key to opening your spirit to newness of life. Forgiveness is a major step toward spiritual growth and development. It must come from the heart, not the mouth. Forgiveness allows us to take off the mask and be free of the negative experiences of anger, pain, disappointment, guilt and shame.

In closing, as you take the step of faith and begin to take off the mask, be willing to not only tell the truth, drop the baggage and forgive others but forgive yourself. Don't allow yourself to walk around deceived by the guilt of the past. When we forgive ourselves and others, we are free to experience love, joy, happiness, success and peace. If you are not receiving good things in your life, you need to forgive. If you're not giving freely and feeling good about it, you need to forgive. If there is anyone you have negative memories about, you need to forgive. Forgiveness is the spiritual laxative that purges the mind, heart and spirit from the toxic events that will constipate you spiritually. Be willing to take the face off and deal with the naked truth about you and all of your issues, once and for all!

I DECLARE WAR

Ephesians 6:12
For we wrestle not against flesh and blood, but against <u>principalities</u>, against <u>powers</u>, against the <u>rulers of the darkness</u> of this world, against <u>spiritual wickedness</u> in high places.

Have you ever been sick and tired of being sick and tired? We all have at one time or another. I am convinced that when you really get sick and tired of your situation, you will do something about it. Today, I want to encourage you to take authority over that which is happening in your life and declare war. The bible tells us as children of GOD to be strong in the Lord, and in the power of his might. Put on the whole armor of God that ye may be able to stand against the wiles of the devil. It is important to note the power and the presence of GOD when you plead the blood. Not the blood found at the American Red Cross. That blood has an expiration date. I'm talking about the blood that was shed on the cross that will never lose its power! It's so powerful it reaches to the highest mountain and it even flows to the lowest valley. The blood will give you strength to keep on fighting in the midst of spiritual warfare.

Don't you back down or punk out to the devil another day. He is already defeated. His purpose is to kill, steal and destroy but the Lord has already ordained you to be more than a conqueror. The fight is fixed. You already have the victory. Don't believe the lies. The bible says in I Peter 5:8, "your adversary the devil, as a roaring lion, walketh about, seeking whom he may devour." He is selling wolf tickets; a bunch of hot air to make you feel intimidated, timid and afraid. Don't you dare sleep on the enemy! It's time to declare war! Matthew 16:19 "and I will give unto thee the keys to the kingdom of heaven: and whatsoever thou shalt bind on earth shall be bound in heaven: and whatsoever thou shalt loose on earth shall be loosed in heaven."

It's time to fight the good fight of faith, with the Word of GOD. Be confident that you are what the Word says you are and you can do what the Word says you can do. Use these principles below to fight as you now declare war on the enemy of your soul. Say them aloud and speak each of them with authority! You can decree a thing and it shall be established! I DECLARE WAR!

> I am - a child of God (Romans 8:16)
> I am - redeemed from the hand of the enemy (Psalm 107:2)
> I am - exercising my authority over the enemy (Luke 10:19)
> I am- above only and not beneath (Deuteronomy 28:13)
> I am - more than a conqueror (Romans 8:37)
> I am - an overcomer by the blood of the lamb and the Word of my testimony (Revelation 12:11)
> I am - daily overcoming the devil, because the greater One lives in me (I John 4:4)
> I am - not moved by what I see (II Corinthians 4:18)
> I am - walking by faith and not by sight (II Corinthians 5:7)
> I am - forgiven (Colossians 1:13, 14)
> I am - saved by grace through faith (Ephesians 2:8)
> I am – justified (excused for something done) (Romans 5:1)
> I am - sanctified (free from sin, pure and holy) (I Corinthians 6:11)
> I am - a new creature in Christ; old things are passed away! (II Corinthians 5:17)
> I am - a partaker of His divine nature (II Peter 1:4)
> I am - delivered from the powers of darkness (Colossians 1:13)
> I am - led by the Spirit of God (Romans 8:14)
> I am - free from all bondage (John 8:36)
> I am - kept in safety wherever I go (Psalm 91:11)
> I am - getting all my needs met by Jesus (Philippians 4:19)

I am - casting all my cares on Jesus (I Peter 5:7)
I am - doing all things through Christ who strengthens me (Philippians 4:13)
I am - an heir of God and a joint heir with Jesus (Romans 8:17)
I am - heir to the blessings of Abraham (Galatians 3:13, 14)
I am – observing and doing the Lord's commandments (Deuteronomy 28:12)
I am - blessed coming in and blessed going out (Deuteronomy 28:6)
I am - an heir of eternal life (I John 5:11, 12)
I am - blessed with all spiritual blessings (Ephesians 1:3)
I am - healed by his stripes (I Peter 2:24)
I am - casting down vain imaginations, ideas and thoughts (II Corinthians 10:4, 5)
I am - strong in the Lord and in the power of His might (Ephesians 6:10)
I declare war!!!

3

THE JORDAN RIVER - "EXHALTATION"

YOU'RE NOT TRASH BUT TREASURE!

Matt 21:42 & Ps. 118:22-23
"The stone which the builders rejected has become the chief cornerstone: this is the Lord's doing, and it is marvelous in our eyes?"
2 Cor. 4:7
"But we have this treasure in earthen vessels, that the excellency of the power may be of God, and not of us."

Many men and women in our community have gone through various situations in life, such as periods of incarceration, addictions, abuse, neglect, abandonment and the list goes on and on. Often, unresolved issues can cause one to become stigmatized or should I say ostracized as a "social outcast". This leaves them feeling as if they have no value, are worthless, useless, pointless, inferior, or discarded like trash. As children of God, we have to remind ourselves that we are not what we have been through. The enemy would have us to believe that we are never going to be successful because of our past experiences. I want to encourage you on today that this simply is not true. You're not trash but treasure!

In our text, it describes a stone that once was rejected and counted as nothing but somehow became the chief cornerstone. Webster's defines the word stone as a gem or precious stone; harden earthly or mineral matter; rock or dirt. That's interesting considering we were formed from the dust of the earth. Could it be that we are the very stone in the text that has been rejected? The word rejected means to discard as defective or useless. Rejection can also be defined as a sense of being unwanted or excluded; always on the outside looking in. Last but not least, the word cornerstone is a stone at the corner of a building uniting two intersecting walls; a principal person; distinguished.

After taking an in-depth look at these definitions, I began to think about the process of a diamond. Did you know that before it is ever recognized for its true worth and value, it doesn't look like much in its original state? To the eye, it is rough, dirty and just a blob of a hardened earthly substance called carbon. Oftentimes, we walk over it, kick it to the side, reject it, or take it for granted. Like that diamond, many of you have found yourself stuck in a hardened, rejected state, bound by the residue of past failures and issues. These things hinder your ability to really "bling-bling" or shine and be all that God has ordained for your life.

You are not alone. We have all been let down, disappointed, rejected and lied to. When you surrender your life to the Lord and allow Him to take you through the process of purification, you like that diamond will begin to see your true worth and value. In life, it's not how you start but how you finish. Be determined to live a life full of purpose and power because you are not trash but a treasure. God gave of His only priceless Son for you and me. That says a lot about you and the investment God made in you before you were even formed in your mother's womb, which was before you ever committed a sin. Walk boldly and confidently into the promises of God. Your playing small does not serve the world. Never shrink back so others will feel comfortable. Let them take their personal stuff up with GOD. You are not trash but a treasure!

MAKING OF A CHAMPION

Genesis 50:20
"But as for you, ye thought evil against me; but God meant it unto good, to bring to pass, as it is this day, to save much people alive."

In our text, I believe Joseph was a champion. He was a man who had a vision. He had the mind-set and was determined **not** to allow what he was going through to break his spirit or rob him of his DREAM! He survived everything that the enemy set against him and he prospered. He could have given up on what GOD showed him in a vision when he found himself lying in a pit. He could have become so depressed that he decided to just kill himself because it seemed like life was not going to get any better. Friends walked away and family turned their backs but Joseph did not give in to the situation that was going on around him. He allowed the situation to make him better. Did you catch that? Better not BITTER! **Better Not Bitter!**

When you look at his life, you'll note that he was Favored by GOD. The very hand of the LORD was upon his life. However, although he was favored by GOD and loved by his father, he was hated by his brothers. They were jealous. They plotted to kill him, stripped him of his colorful jacket, threw him in a pit and sold him into slavery for 20 shekels of silver. He was bought by Potipher as a slave and moved in Potipher's house. Potipher's wife tried to holla at him on the low. She became angry and made a decision to set him up. She cried rape and the next thing you know, Joseph was in jail. I am not making this up. Read the text. You will see the whole story for yourself.

Joseph went through pure hell but he made it back from all of that DRAMA! The making of a CHAMPION! Webster defines a champion as one that holds first place or wins first prize in a contest or competition; one that is clearly superior or has the attributes of a winner. Being the scholar that I am, I have taken the authority to define the word myself. I believe that a champion is an individual who has the ability to see past their current state. Obtain a vision for your life. Endure, persevere and overcome obstacles, setbacks and hindrances like a good solider in order to fulfill your God-given potential, purpose and destiny. *In other words, a champion is an individual who knows how to take a lickin' and keep on tickin'. A champion is a survivor!*

With that in mind, could it be that the things you are going through are somehow, some way working for your good? Sometimes in life, you may have to be torn down to your lowest in order to be built up! When skyscrapers are in the process of being built, the workers have to dig deep in order to build a foundation that is built to last. Whether you realize it or not, you have been built to last! That's the only reason you haven't lost your mind. You've been built to last. Who else could survive the conditions you've been forced to live in at this time? Give yourself credit. It takes a lot to survive mentally, emotionally and physically the things you have had to endure. Could this chapter in your life be the very training ground that is making you into a champion? I believe you have the spirit of Joseph. You've been through all kinds of stuff! To look at you, nobody would know the hell you had to endure. Nobody really knows about the stuff from childhood that you couldn't talk about. People think they know you but they really don't. You laugh and talk and act like everything is okay but the truth is you sometimes want to cry, but you can't! You have gotten so use to wearing the mask in order to function from day-to-day.

Allow me to encourage you to keep on pressing. Your labor is not in vain. One day, you will be able to say it was good for me that I was afflicted! It was good that I had to go through that in order to get to this. I understand now that the situation was for my good and for His glory! Like Marvin Sapp, you too can sing, "I am stronger, wiser and so much better." No matter what you do, don't let the things you are going through make you bitter. Allow the stuff to make you better. On the other side of this, after it's all said and done, you can look back and say like Joseph in Genesis 50:20 "but as for you, ye thought evil against me; but God meant it unto good, to bring to pass, as it is this day, to save much people alive." The making of a champion!

I AM A COMEBACK KID!

John 11: 39, 43-44

39 Jesus said, Take ye away the stone. Martha, the sister of him that was dead, saith unto him, Lord, by this time he stinketh: for he hath been dead four days.
43 And when he thus had spoken, he cried with a loud voice, Lazarus, come forth.
44 And he that was dead came forth, bound hand and foot with grave clothes: and his face was bound about with a napkin. Jesus saith unto them, Loose him, and let him go.

Webster's dictionary defines a comeback kid as a person who overcomes a fall from grace or popularity; a person who makes an unlikely return. In other words, a comeback kid is an individual who, against all odds, obstacles and set backs have survived the enemy's hardest hit! They are like that of the timex, they have learned how to take a lickin' but keep right on tickin'!

On the other hand, there are some of you who don't feel as though you are a comeback kid because like Lazarus, you have found yourself in a stinky situation. Feeling like Hannah, you're a woman or man of a sorrowful spirit. It seems like the more you pray and believe God for your breakthrough, the more it keeps right on happening for everybody else. You cried, you prayed, you fasted and nothing! Perhaps your stinky situation is the result of a doctor's report. Maybe you're filled with grief, frustration and the truth is, you're angry! You are feeling forsaken by friends and family. You may even at times feel forsaken by God.

It may feel like the enemy has the upper hand on you but don't give up! Fight your way to the promise with everything you have left in you. As a child, Glow- (gorgeous ladies of wrestling) was one of my favorite television shows. I loved to use my vivid imagination as if I were Mt. Fuji, the Hawaiian dominator. She was my kind of girl. When it was time to fight, she didn't allow the temporary discomfort to get the upper hand. I would watch how she would rest during the time her opponent was rejoicing over what she thought was going to be her demise. Although the referee was in the midst of the 10 count, trying to determine if she was going to be physically able to finish the fight, she always found a way to make a comeback, no matter what.

Yes, on today, your enemies may be counting you out for one reason or the other, but rest assured that according to Micah 7:8 you will make a comeback. "⁸ rejoice not against me, o mine enemy: when I fall, I shall arise;" I believe our text teaches us a powerful lesson on the survival of stinky situations. Here are 3 keys for making a comeback!

First things first, you have to believe. Look at verse 25. Jesus said, "I am the resurrection, and the life: he that believeth in me, though he were dead, yet shall he live." The enemy will try to play on your mind to get you to doubt God and His ability! He would love to make you believe that the Lord is not concerned about you. That simply is not true! In verse 5 of this same chapter, we see that Jesus loved Lazarus and his sisters, Mary and Martha. Although He loved them, they too found themselves in a stinky situation. You've got to settle the issue of doubt in your mind and believe what the Word of God says about you and your situation. Don't be moved by what you see. Believe! One sister in the text was tripping, saying to Jesus, "If you would have been here, he would not have died." Don't be like that sister. When tragedy comes, believe God, no matter what.

Why should you believe in the midst of the problem? Because your belief system will keep you from fainting, according to Psalm 27:13 "I had fainted, unless had believed to see the goodness of the lord in the land of the living." In addition, your belief system attacks fear. Mark 5:36, "Be not afraid, only believe." Luke 8:50 "Jesus said, fear not: believe only, and she shall be made whole." Your belief system also ignites your faith, Mark 9:23 "Jesus said unto him, if thou canst believe, all things are possible to him that believeth." Finally, your belief system will produce results according to Mark 11:24 "Therefore I say unto you, what things soever ye desire, when ye pray, believe that ye receive them, and ye shall have them."

Secondly, if you're going to be a comeback kid in this season, you must maintain your ability to hear. The bible says he that hath an ear, let him hear. Faith comes by hearing and hearing by Word of God! Don't let the sound of your dilemma drown out the voice of God speaking to you concerning your situation. You've got to make it up in your mind that you might be going through but you have made a decision to maintain your ability to hear from God! Look at verse 43 "and when he thus had spoken, he cried with a loud voice, Lazarus, come forth 44 and he that was dead came forth, bound hand and foot with grave clothes: his face was bound with a napkin." Notice that he was still bound by a stinky situation but he heard something. I wonder what would have happened if he had lost his sense of hearing. Would he have missed his divine opportunity to be delivered and set free? Maintain your ear to hear. Listen to Him speaking specifically to you through His Word, through other people and even through your circumstances. Block out the chatter and worry in your mind. Hear God.

Last but not least, you must maintain the ability to respond to the voice of God. In the text, Jesus instructed Lazarus to come forth. In order to get free, Lazarus responded to the specific instructions. He was bound by the situation but he responded in faith, not based on his condition. Are you willing to respond to the voice of God who has the power to change your stinky situation or are you going to remain in the same stinky hopeless situation? Notice that it wasn't until after he had heard the voice of Jesus and he began to move that Jesus commanded the grave clothes, the very thing that had him bound to loose him and let him go! By the authority invested in me, I speak to every situation that has had you bound. I command them to loose you now and let you go! The past is the past! You are a comeback kid!!!

Jesus was not concerned about Lazarus' past and why he ended up in that situation. He was determined not to allow him to stay in that situation! The bible is full of stories of people like you and me with a past but who managed to make a comeback. With that in mind, I decree and declare: **YOU ARE A COMEBACK KID!**

A PECULIAR PEOPLE

1 Peter 2:9
But ye are a chosen generation, a royal priesthood, an holy nation, a peculiar people; that ye should shew forth the praises of him who hath <u>called</u> you out of darkness into his marvelous light;

Many times, we have tried to fit into what society would call normal or average when we were never meant to be any of those things. According to the Word of God found in I Peter 2:9, looking at the adjectives, it describes both you and me. We are chosen. Chosen is defined as hand picked; selected; royal; defined as regal; set apart; held to a high standard; or a holy nation; a group of people who have been set apart to God for a purpose. A peculiar people means for *God's* own possession or differing from the world. The term peculiar is defined as strange; queer; odd; uncommon; unusual; distinctive in nature or character from others.

I am reminded of a very popular movie, "Forest Gump". The main character, Forest, is often referred to as everything but a child of God. Many thought he was rather odd, dumb and even plain foolish or strange. However, he never allowed other's perception of him to change who he really was. His mother instilled in him principles that caused him to rise above the world's limitations. As a peculiar individual, he went to a good school, became a football hero, served his country in Vietnam, met very important people, including the president, invented the smiley face logo, started a fitness craze running all over the world, became a shrimp tycoon and even helped his disgruntled friend, Lt. Dan, come to Lord where he found faith and peace.

My question to you is simply this: Are you still trying to fit in or are you busy fulfilling your God-ordained purpose in the earth?

Like Forrest Gump, we have been chosen for greatness. The bible is full of peculiar people who did great things in the earth. What are you waiting for? You can not afford to sit back another day being comfortable with just being average. Being comfortable with average will never give birth to the greatness on the inside of you.

GOD has called each and every one of us to be peculiar. He has equipped us with the necessary skills to conquer the giants in us and around us. There is tenacity in each of us. That's the stuff that makes you run past the pain and discomfort to see the plan through to the end. You have resilience. That's the courage that makes you get up when you fall down, get back in the race, and keep fighting all the way to the finish line. In conclusion, know that you have favor, the unmerited grace of GOD to see you through. Favor allows you to jump over hurdles, avoid obstacles, setbacks and hindrances to make all of your dreams come true! People of God, it's your time to tap into the Peculiar! You have a right to live the life Jesus died for you to have. Don't settle. You are PECULIAR!

IT'S POSSIBLE SERIES

Judges 4: 1-3 & Judges 5:7
¹And the children of Israel again did evil in the sight of the LORD, when Ehud was dead. ²And the LORD sold them into the hand of Jabin king of Canaan, that reigned in Hazor; the captain of whose host was Sisera, which dwelt in Harosheth of the Gentiles. ³And the children of Israel cried unto the LORD: for he had nine hundred chariots of iron; and twenty years he mightily oppressed the children of Israel.
Judges 5: 7 *"The inhabitants of the villages ceased, they ceased in Israel, until that I Deborah arose..."*

RISE UP!

Today, the focus is on the life of Deborah and the lessons she taught. Deborah was a woman who like many of you had been living in a state of oppression for many years. Oppression is defined as cruelty or abuse of power and authority. This is a condition that will have you feeling as though something is weighing so heavily on your mind that it seems to be stopping or blocking you from doing and being what God has called you to be. We see your glory but no one really knows your story. No one knows the personal oppression that you have had to endure. No one knows about the disappointments, unfavorable doctor's reports, and all the stuff that just seems to hover over you.

Don't just sit here and die. Arise! I say to you today, like Jesus did in Mark 5:41. I speak to some dead, oppressed situations; Damsel arise! Arise out of that state of oppression because enough is enough. Arise out of that place of frustration because enough is enough. Arise from that place of agitation because enough is enough. Arise up out of the stress because enough is enough. You better look at the devil and say, it was a good hit but you couldn't take me out. I have a right to arise. You better know that you have the right to live the life that Jesus died for you to have! ARISE!

MY LIFE IS CHOICE-DRIVEN

In Judges 4, we see where the children of Israel did evil. So, God sold them into slavery, bondage, and oppression. It is here that I began my argument with the text. How could a loving and merciful God sell His people out to the enemy? How could He allow them to live in bondage? How could He just allow them to live in a state of cruel and ruthless oppression for 20 years? After studying the book of Judges, it became pretty clear to me why God did what He did. The Israelites did exactly what they wanted to do. The bible says that everyone did what was right in their own eyes. This is very similar to people today doing exactly what they want to do without any reverence for God. You know that mentality that it's my thing and I will do what I want to do. It is here that I understood why the hard-headed Israelites were put into bondage. They began to live among idolaters and became contaminated with false Gods. They began to participate in idolatry and things that separated them from the true and the living God. So, my question to you is, could it be our behaviors, issues, choices, and lifestyles that separate us from our divine possibilities? Could it be our stuff that separates us from the move of God in our lives causing us not to experience the miraculous? If that is the case, then there is still hope.

Believe it or not, your life is choice-driven. You will live or die as a result of the choices that you make. The text speaks about our choices and how we can turn back to GOD after having made a bad choice. II Chronicles 7:14 "If my people, which are called by my name, shall humble themselves, and pray, and seek my face, and turn from their wicked ways; then will I hear from heaven, and forgive their sin, and will heal their land." He said turn from your wicked ways. That means to denounce it, to get rid of it, and to stop doing the stuff over again. Only then will He hear from heaven, forgive sin, and heal the land!

I CHANGED MY MIND, HE RESTORED ME!

If you are going to tap into the divine possibility, you will be required to change your mind, your way of thinking and your behaviors. Judges 4:3 spoke to me because the children of Israel knew that they were in trouble. They were not crazy or in denial about it. Yet, they had enough sense to change their minds and cry out to God for help. Have you ever cried out to God and He delivered you? He healed you and brought you out but then you went right back to the same situation. You got tied up and tangled up all over again; tangled up in a yoke of bondage! The good news is Jeremiah 33:3 says, "Call unto me, and I will answer thee, and show thee great and mighty thing."

When you mess up or disappoint people, they are not obligated to answer your calls or to deal with you anymore. However, I thank and praise a mighty God that even though He is able to see my mess, He looks beyond all of my faults and answers every time I call. Like me, you may have messed up a time or two, but you can change your mind. In changing your mind, you totally surrender to the will of God for your life. In surrendering to God, you allow Him to transform your mind once and for all. Then, you will be able to prove what is that good and acceptable thing for your life. It is not until your mind has been changed that you cry out to God and when He brings you out, you stay out, you stay delivered, and you stay set free. That is why you have to change your mind.

The Israelites had enough sense to cry out to God. It was when they cried out that He restored them. Do you know about the power of restoration? See, when I should have been cut off, disqualified, written off and counted as nothing because of my mess, I cried out to God and He restored me! Yes, people may know a little about your past. They may hold it against you but GOD will restore you. He will restore your soul. Galatians 6:1

declares: "Brethren, if a man be overtaken in a fault, ye which are spiritual, restore such a one in the spirit of meekness; considering thyself, lest thou also be tempted." I wonder what would happen if the body of Christ got back to the basics and began restoring people. What would really happen if we started restoring people back into their positions in God? I believe that if we who are spiritual would begin to restore people, they would gain the strength to tell the devil, No, not today because I have changed my mind! They will look at the crack pipe and say, No, you can not hold me hostage anymore because I have changed my mind. If we restore them, they will gain the strength to look at the caller ID and say, I have changed my mind.

IDENTIFY YOUR PURPOSE

Many times, we get caught up in the wrong stuff. We seek validation and approval from other people before we step out and do what God has told us to do. Not Deborah. In Judges 4:4-5, we see that Deborah was a woman who was focused. She was focused and determined to fulfill her purpose in the earth one way or another. In the text, we find Deborah, a woman of divine possibilities, fulfilling her life's work under a palm tree. She knew what she had on the inside of her could not be stopped or hindered by the religious dogma, religious system, or the opinion of others. In that day, it was unlawful for a woman to be in the synagogue alone with a man. Deborah said, "Look, let me tell you something. What I'm carrying is bigger then a synagogue. I'll take it to the streets." Like Deborah, you don't need an office, a pulpit or an official title to fulfill your purpose. There are souls on the line and it's time to identify your purpose and walk in it. You can not allow your destiny to be stopped or hindered because people don't think you're qualified. Be confident that you have been justified.

In Judges, we see Deborah out there making it happen. She was out there serving the people in the community as a judge. A judge was similar to a mediator or counselor. People went to Deborah because she provided sound wisdom. Deborah identified her purpose and maintained her position in the kingdom. When you are in your set place, where God has called you, anything is possible! Did not the Word tell us in Deut. 28 that when you harken unto the voice of the Lord your God and obey his statues, blessed shall you be in the city, and blessed shall you be in the field? Don't you let anyone talk you out of your purpose.

YOUR RIGHT TO EMPOWER YOUR BELIEF

When we look at Judges 4:6-8, we see that Deborah had received instructions from God. She spoke to Barak and told him exactly what thus said the Lord, as instructed. However, fear set in and Barak said, "No, Deborah. I am not going. I am not going unless you go." Deborah knew that she wasn't responsible for his response. Deborah was a bad girl! In Judges 4:9, she responded to his cry with authority! She said, "Look, Barak I will go with you but I'm going to tell you one thing for certain and two things for sure. The battle will be given into the hand of a woman." Like Deborah, you have to learn the art of empowering your own belief system. Deborah believed in her GOD and her ability. She knew that she had what it took to pursue, overtake, and recover all! So, you have to empower your own belief system and do what God has called you to do.

It is your belief system that gives you the courage to face all of your fears with faith. It is your belief system that gives you the ability to conquer the giants in your life. That is why you have to empower your own belief system. The bible did say that we could decree a thing and it shall be established. So, what are you using your mouth piece for? Are you decreeing the Word of God? Don't you know that angels are on assignment ascending and descending to and from heaven coming for your words? When you begin to decree, you set the atmosphere in motion for what you believe God for. Start empowering your belief system with words of affirmation. When the enemy tries to attack me, I like to use affirmations and confessions of faith to remind the enemy of my rights as a child of GOD. Allow me to quickly remind you of your rights:

1. You have the right to wake up and live the life of your dreams!

2. You have a right to enjoy today and believe that tomorrow will be better than today!
3. You have a right to pursue your dreams and accomplish every one of your goals!
4. You have a right to face and transform your fears with courage and with faith!
5. You have a right to break the glass ceiling and live beyond the limits!
6. You have a right to stop being all things to everybody because you have the right to nurture yourself like you nurture others!
7. You have a right to take your moments to fill up your own cup first and replenish others from your overflow!
8. You have a right to live within your means and not even try to keep up with the Jones'.
9. You have a right to prosper beyond your imagination; to insist on being paid fairly for what you do!
10. You have a right to complete unfinished business!
11. You have a right to view your failures in life as lessons!
12. You have a right to choose success over every failure!
13. You have a right to turn your loses into gains!
14. You have a right to give yourself credit, to love the little girl in you, to be a friend to yourself, to be good to yourself and to be totally honest with yourself about yourself!
15. You have a right to say NO and mean it! Knowing that NO is a full sentence with no explanations needed!
16. You have a right to heal old and current wounds!
17. You have a right to make forgiveness your number one priority!
18. You have a right to develop healthy and supportive relationships!
19. You have a right to know that you are loveable!
20. You have a right to love unconditionally!

21. You have a right as a single lady to be alone without feeling lonely!
22. You have a right to stop being a trash can and a dumping bin for other people's junk!
23. You have a right to rid yourself of toxic relationships and to take an emotional enema when necessary!
24. You have a right to laugh out loud, live out loud, to play as hard as you can, and to dance like nobody is watching!
25. You have a right to sing at the top of your voice and to color outside of the lines!
26. You have a right to rise, to pursue, to overtake, and to recover all!
27. You have a right to do all of these things because you are full of divine possibilities!

In closing, if you know that you have rights, I want you to decree some things out loud. Say, "I will pray and expect an exceptional and favorable outcome because I have a right to. I will wave goodbye to guilt, self-doubt, rejection, jealousy, and insecurity. I will live, learn, love, serve and then, leave a legacy."

ENGAGE IN SPIRITUAL WARFARE: FIGHT!

Make no mistake, the enemy has studied you and he doesn't want you to tap into your divine possibilities. However, you have to declare war! He has all kinds of demons in place ready to attempt to attack you. You better know that the bible says we wrestle not against flesh and blood but against principalities, powers, rulers of darkness of this world, and spiritual wickedness in high places.
We have to give the devil credit. He is organized. This is why God tells us in Ephesians 6:11 to "Put on the whole armor of God, that ye may be able to stand against the wiles of the devil." When you are in warfare, you have to know how to plead the Blood! Now, don't get it twisted. I'm not talking about the blood from the American Red Cross because that blood has an expiration date.
I'm talking about the Blood that never loses its power; the Blood that reaches to the highest mountain and flows to the lowest valley. You have a right to plead the Blood that gives you strength from day-to-day.

Don't you punk out to the devil another day because you have a right to engage in spiritual warfare. So, draw a line in the sand and say enough is enough. You need to be like Deborah and say I declare war. See, as they were going out to the battle, Deborah knew that the timing and the strategy of God were very important.
When you are in warfare, you can step out there and do it your way if you want to. While you are all in the flesh, you will get jacked up like the sons of Sceva! However, when you do it the way God says to do it, even when it doesn't make sense, He will bring you through to victory every single time!

In Judges 4:10, they only had ten thousand men and a prophetess by the name of Deborah. Yet, they defeated nine hundred chariots of iron. Those nine hundred chariots had oppressed the children of Israel for 20 years but they were given the victory because they did it GOD's way. In Judges 4:17, the commander-in-chief who had been oppressing the children of Israel for 20 years was now running scared. If he was so big and bad, why in the world is he running? He was running from the situation. However, in the midst of his running, there was another woman of divine possibility on the scene by the name of Jael. She knew that Sisera was not right. However, she was polite to him because he was cool with her husband. So, in Judges 4:18, she invited him into her house and gave him milk to drink. Then Sisera went to sleep. (He was not wrapped too tight.) How was he going to oppress and kill people left and right and then have the unmitigated gall to go into Jael's house and go to sleep? Here he was, the root of all the oppression, asleep in the house of Jael in Judges 4:21.

This leads me to to my final point. Jael went off! She took that hammer and tent nail and drove it through his head and into the ground. That was some kind of hit! I want you to take on the spirit of Jael and take the heel of your shoe and drive it through the head of Satan. You have a right to give him a migraine headache! Better yet, give him an aneurysm with your praise! See, every time you pick your feet up and put them down, you remind Satan of his position in your life, which is under your feet!

You have a right to praise and thank your God! He brought you out of darkness into the marvelous light. You have a right to praise because you are saved, healed, and delivered. You have a right to praise because you changed your mind and you have identified your purpose. The devil may have held you up for maybe 20 sec, 20 min, 20 days, 20 months or like Deborah, for 20 years. However, I double-dog dare you to give God glory and to give the devil a nightmare. You have a right to praise because you are full of divine possibilities. What's to come in your life is better than what has been. Tap into your possibilities. Don't allow the issues of your life to oppress you another day. If the devil thinks that you are something now, just wait because the bible says that it does not yet appear what you shall be! It's possible.

4

THE RIVER EURPHATES - "PROVISION"

I'M STEPPING INTO MY CHANGE

Mark 5:25-29
25And a certain woman, which had an issue of blood twelve years, 26And had suffered many things of many physicians, and had spent all that she had, and was nothing bettered, but rather grew worse, 27When she had heard of Jesus, came in the press behind, and touched his garment. 28For she said, If I may touch but his clothes, I shall be whole. 29 And straightway the fountain of her blood was dried up; and she felt in her body that she was healed of the plague.

The R& B legend, SAM Cook, said "It's been a long, long time coming but I know a change is going to come!" This woman in our text had been waiting a long time for a change. The bible said she had been struggling for twelve years. Can you even imagine dealing with this same problem, same issue, fighting the same battle for twelve years? That's 4,380 days. She had to have been sick and tired of being sick and tired. In observing her actions in this text, she taught a very powerful lesson on the how to step into a change. I believe her actions are prophetic to the ways in which we can step out of one season in our lives into another. The first thing she did to step into a change was 1. Recognize the solution. Right there in the midst of the suffering, she recognized that if anyone could handle this issue of hers, Jesus could. Recognition is one of the major keys to your change. Recognize the greater One that lives on the inside of you and His ability to bring you through any problem.

The second thing she did was 2. Activate her Faith and Confessed the word. Note this woman's faith in verse 28, "For she said, If I may touch but his clothes, I shall be whole." She had to have seen herself healed in the midst of the issue. She saw the healing and then began to SPEAK it out of her mouth into existence. If this woman had the faith to activate a miracle in her life, what's your excuse? The bible says you can DECREE a thing and it shall be established. When you begin to speak the Word of God over your life, it sets the atmosphere in motion for that which you have spoken to come to pass. Did you not know that angels are ascending and descending to and from heaven? They are coming for your words? They are on an assignment to assist you but are you giving them anything to work with? It's time to Decree some things you have been believing God for.

Finally, she 3. Took action and received her promise. Take a look at verse 27. "When she had heard of Jesus, came in the press behind, and touched his garment." Her faith has now overpowered all of her fears and has set her up to receive the very promises of GOD. As soon as she took action, she came in the press behind him and SUDDENLY, her issue or situation CHANGED! 29"And straightway the fountain of her blood was dried up; and she felt in her body that she was healed of that plague." She stepped into a change.

On today, you like this woman in the text, may feel like you have been struggling with an issue for years now. Things don't appear to have gotten any better but worse. I encourage you to press into the presence of GOD and allow the healing virtue of Jesus to heal you of your issue. Allow him to heal you once and for all so that you might step into your CHANGE.

THE GREAT INVESTMENT

Acts 9: 5, 15-18

5 And he said, Who art thou, Lord? And the Lord said, I am Jesus whom thou persecutest: it is hard for thee to kick against the pricks.
15 But the Lord said unto him, Go thy way: for he is a chosen vessel unto me, to bear my name before the Gentiles, and kings, and the children of Israel: 16 For I will shew him how great things he must suffer for my name's sake. 17 And Ananias went his way, and entered into the house; and putting his hands on him said, Brother Saul, the Lord, even Jesus, that appeared unto thee in the way as thou camest, hath sent me, that thou mightest receive thy sight, and be filled with the Holy Ghost. 18 And immediately there fell from his eyes as it had been scales: and he received sight forthwith, and arose, and was baptized.

Many GREAT investments have been made at a time when it appeared that it was not wise to do so. Financial Brokers with insight, experience, and discernment will often take risks that others will not take. Theses brokers are distinguished as the aggressive investors who often receive BIG RETURNS! Why, because they are risk-takers or individuals who are willing to step out of their comfort zone. In our text, Jesus, the Stockbroker, for the purpose of this sermon, has stepped out of His ordinary comfort zone and is now assessing and observing the current and potential stock market. In verses 1 & 2, Saul, the enemy to the current stock (Body of Christ) has been found guilty of persecuting the Christians with the ultimate goal to destroy all that called upon the Lord. Notice in the text, although Saul was an enemy, Jesus referred to him as a "chosen vessel". Like Saul, we all have been found guilty of participating in some type of sinful activity that was not pleasing to GOD.

Unlike man, who will count you out based on your past failures, GOD has chosen to invest in the lives of sinners for His glory. All throughout the bible, we see the hand of GOD on the lives of ordinary people with not so pleasant pasts. Noah was a man with issues, an alcoholic, a known public drunk but GOD invested in him and used him for His glory. Moses was a convicted felon. He snapped, kill a man, committed first degree murder but GOD used him for his GLORY. Sampson had his issues and got caught-up with Delilah. Rehab was a prostitute. Peter was violent. He should have been in anger-management based on the way he would curse and carry on. He even cut a man's ear off but the hand of the Lord was yet upon him. David was an adulterer and a murderer. He had a baby out of wedlock. However, he was called a man after God's own heart. Last but not least, you were a whole lot of things. We all have sinned and come short of the glory of GOD!

The good news is GOD has made an investment in you. This investment was made before you were even formed in your mothers' womb. Let me encourage you on today that the past is the past! There is nothing that you have done that has caused the investment Jesus made for you on the cross to crash. Even with your flaws, God desires to use you, your life and your story for His glory! Don't you dare allow the enemy of your soul to rob you of your future by haunting you with guilt, shame and condemnation. I John 1: 9 "If we confess our sins, he is a faithful and just God to forgive us our sins and to cleanse us from all unrighteousness."

The same way Saul had a Damascus road conversion, God so desires to do a new thing in you. Saul was transformed by the renewing of his mind. He went from being a Christian-killer to a powerful man of God by the name of Paul. The same God who invested in the life of Saul has invested in you. You can be saved today! You can be healed today! You can be set free today! All you have to do is come to Him. He will save your soul and fill you with the Holy Ghost. He will start you on a brand new road. All you have to do is come to Him. No matter what you have done, Jesus is the One who will forgive all of your sins. Don't you wait another day. Make a decision to come to Him. You are worth it! You are a GREAT INVESTMENT!

GO TO YOUR WEALTHY PLACE

Psalms 112:3 *Wealth and riches shall be in his house: and his righteousness endureth for ever.*

Have you ever found yourself frustrated as a tither and a giver, frustrated that you're not walking in your wealthy place, frustrated because you're living paycheck to paycheck; robbing Peter to pay Paul. Come on and be honest. Tithers and givers do get frustrated about their financial situations. Webster defines wealth as an abundance of valuable material possessions or resources; the state of being rich; affluence or prosperous; successful; well-to-do; or favorable. Notice the definition did not say that your wealthy place had to be "millionaire status". It did not say that you were wealthy if you drove a certain car, lived in a certain neighborhood, lived in house or apartment.

On the other hand, abundance is defined as having enough to meet your needs and financial obligations with overflow or money left over. Wealth can be achieved regardless of your current economic status. It's about your willingness to apply the principles and use discipline. Wealth and success is an intentional process. It doesn't just happen. You have to work towards it! The bible says faith without works is dead. In addition to tithes and sowing seeds, you are required to do some practical things in order to go to your wealthy place. For starters, you must pay off the past, manage the present and then prepare for the future. The key to getting to where you're going is to know where you're starting from. You need to find the dot that says, "You are here," just like the dot on the kiosk map in the shopping mall. Many people are like hamsters on a treadmill, moving and moving for the sake of movement. Yet, they never really get anywhere because they haven't shifted their mindset.

In the society in which we live, we don't have a problem with income. Rather, we have a problem with managing the money that we have. We all know that we pay for what we love and desire. According to the latest edition of the buying power of Black America, African-Americans' total earned income reached approx. $679 billion. The article reported that the top five things that this money was spent on were: *$53.8 billion on food, $28.7 billion on cars, $22 billion on apparel products & services, $17.9 billion on health care, and $16.6 billion on insurance.* The truth is that much of our spending and overspending has been the result of mimicking what we have seen on tv advisements and in or on others, all for the sake of being perceived as wealthy, when in fact this is not wealth but debt! This is a form of bondage. Overspending is a symptom and not a cause. It is a symptom of a bigger and deeper issue than debt. I would like to help each of you to go to your wealthy place.

First and foremost, you must examine your spending habits to see if you can understand the real reason why your mailbox is full of bills; bills that you have no idea how you're going to pay; bills that are the result of things that you may or may not even remember purchasing. Here is another truth. Your ability to handle money is often a reflection of your security and wholeness as a person. Some women tend to overspend in a fit of fury over a recent breakup with a boyfriend. Others purchase things they can not afford because they feel inferior to others or are trying to impress them. Some people are in debt because they are so deeply wounded by traumas of the past and shopping becomes a way to medicate the pain. Then again, we occasionally see a relatively whole, stable person who simply has a problem with impulse control and delayed gratification. They typically have lots of credit cards and debt!

The truth of the matter is that there is nothing that you can bring home in a shopping bag that can heal the hurts and wounds within. It may numb the pain for a short while or like a drug, take you on a high but the real issues always begin to throb and manifest themselves again and again. Ask yourself:

- Am I an emotional spender?
- What emotions trigger the desire to buy something?
- Have you overextended yourself in order to buy things that you think will impress others or make you feel that people like or accept you?
- Have you gotten yourself into debt trying to buy things that will make you feel better about yourself?
- Have you ever spent money you did not have?
- Have you ever used the overdraft protection plan to make purchases for things that you knew you could not afford?
- Have you ever written checks knowing you did not have the money to cover the check? Then, you play the game of I did not know that the check bounced! I thought I was going to beat the check to the bank!
- Tell the truth, be honest. Has your debt ever exceeded your income and ability to pay?
- Is your credit out of control, so much so that you can't buy anything on credit!

Even if you answered yes to one, some or all of these questions, you still have potential. Go to your wealthy place! I want to encourage you today to go deep within yourself and to get honest with you about you and your financial situation. It may take a while to sort things out but be willing to look at the man in the mirror. Only when you understand yourself, what motivates your spending and the reasons for your spending can you begin to destroy the vicious cycles and harmful patterns in your life. It is at that moment of honesty that we become open-minded and willing to change. These changes will produce lasting results that can and will take us to our wealthy place. Below are some practical principles to help you go through the process to your wealthy place.

1. Figure out what you are actually spending. It is important to establish and maintain a budget to track your spending. In addition, it is important to know your debt to income ratio. Paying your bills on time is always a plus and helps to improve your credit score. The bible tells us to owe no man anything but to love them.

2. Define and discern the difference between wants and needs. (If you can't afford it, don't buy it!) The body of Christ should never be guilty of buying our wants then begging for our needs. Your integrity is on the line.

3. Cut the spending. In corporate America, if the income is low and the debts are high, they downsize in order to cut costs. If you cannot afford it, don't buy it. It is time out for trying to keep up with the Jones', looking like you are prosperous and the truth is, you're broke. It makes no sense to wear designer clothes, drive fancy cars and then cannot afford the maintenance. You may have to make some temporary adjustments and endure a moment of discomfort for long-term pleasure. Stay in your lane and be content with where you are and prepare for the future. Don't allow a moment of pleasure to get you in a position you will not be able to maintain. Downsize, if necessary. You can't save your face if you're behind at the same time.

4. Increase your streams of income. It is important to assess your skills and determine if there is an opportunity

for increase. It may require you to go back to school, get a special certification or license to make you more marketable. In addition, perhaps, you have some transferable skills that are of value to others. This can generate additional income.

5. Eliminate debt. The reality of wealth is you cannot build it without credit. If your credit score is not favorable, start today by making a commitment to fix it. It is of utmost importance to establish a debt elimination plan. Plan your work and work your plan. When you fail to plan, by default you are planning to fail! Take time to list your debts. Consider the balances, interest rates, fees, etc to determine which debt you should pay off first. Once you eliminate that debt, don't spend the money. Use that money you were once paying towards another debt on your payback-payoff plan.

6. Build a savings account. Establishing a savings plan creates a cushion for you in the event of an emergency. Many people look to lines of credit and credit cards to bail them out of emergency situations. It's a better idea to start putting a little money back monthly for your savings. Make saving money a priority and commit to not use it unless it is a real emergency.

In closing, stay committed and consistent with your plan, no matter what! If at first you don't succeed, try and try again. It works if you work it, but you've got to work it every day. You are equipped. You are empowered to go to your wealthy place!

5

THE RIVER OF EGYPT - "PROMISES"

PREGNANT WITH A PROMISE

There have been times when we all have gotten a little frustrated. We are living right, believing God, yet what we are experiencing is not lining up with what we have been expecting from God! The frustrations and disappointments of life can oftentimes have you governing your life by quotes like: "Well, stuff just happens." "All good things must come to an end." "If it isn't one thing, it's another." Perhaps you feel that this is as good as it's going to get. Well, this is NOT as good as it gets! The Word of GOD tells us that better is the ending of a thing than the beginning. Why, you might ask? The suffering of this present time is not worthy to be compared with the glory that shall be revealed. You may feel like your life is on hold, waiting for the promise but don't you give up! You have got to hold on to your promise, no matter what!

The truth is you are not alone. Many of us have found ourselves frustrated like Abraham and Sarah, stuck between the prophecy and the promise. All the promises of GOD in him are still yes, and Amen! Some of you may be saying, I have been holding on to this prophecy, this promise for years, and it looks like nothing is happening for me. I Corinthians 15:58 "Be ye steadfast, unmovable, always abounding in the work of the Lord, forasmuch as ye know that your labor is not in vain." A promise is still a promise. It doesn't matter how long you have been waiting! A promise is still a promise.

A promise is defined as a word that goes forth into unfilled time. It reaches ahead of its speaker and its recipient to mark an appointment between them in the future. A promise may be an assurance of continuing or a future action on behalf of someone. A promise can also be defined as a contract, covenant, oath, or pledge; an enforceable agreement between two or more parties. Did you know that the bible is full of PROMISES or covenants between you and GOD? These promises are enforceable but you must know the terms and conditions of the contract; terms like, John 15:7 which says, "If ye abide in me, and my words abide in you, ye shall ask what ye will, and it shall be done." Psalm 84:11 says, "No good thing will he withhold from them that walk uprightly." Deuteronomy 28:2-3 says, "And all these blessing shall come on thee, and overtake thee, if thou shall hearken unto the voice of the LORD thy God. Blessed shall thou be in the city and blessed shall thou be in the field." Ephesians 3:20 says, "God is still able to do exceedingly and abundantly more then you can ever ask or think." You need to know that a promise is still a promise!

THE PROCESS: MARY'S PROMISE

Luke 1:26-31, 34 &35
²⁶And in the sixth month the angel Gabriel was sent from God unto a city of Galilee, named Nazareth, ²⁷To a virgin espoused to a man whose name was Joseph, of the house of David; and the virgin's name was Mary. ²⁸And the angel came in unto her, and said, Hail, thou that art highly favored, the Lord is with thee: blessed art thou among women· ²⁹And when she saw him, she was troubled at his saying, and cast in her mind what manner of salutation this should be. ³⁰And the angel said unto her, Fear not, Mary: for thou hast found favor with God. ³¹And, behold, thou shall conceive in thy womb, and bring forth a son, and shall call his name JESUS.
³⁴Then said Mary unto the angel, how shall this be, seeing I know not a man? ³⁵And the angel answered and said unto her, The Holy Ghost shall come upon thee, and the power of the Highest shall overshadow thee: therefore also that holy thing which shall be born of thee shall be called the Son of God."

In our text, we find this woman, Mary, who like many of you, was pregnant with a promise. This woman teaches a very powerful lesson on the ways and means to endure the process of pregnancy and birthing of the promise. Allow me to give you eight (8) power principles I noted from the life of Mary in Luke 1:26-49:

PRINCIPLE ONE: CALM DOWN!

Luke 1:29 says that Mary was troubled. Let's be honest ladies. At times, we get a little emotional and tend to make irrational decisions out of our feelings rather than faith. In this season of your life, you can not afford to act on emotions. You have to find a way to calm down. Oftentimes, we make situations worse due to our levels of stress and anxieties. We have to calm down and understand that God has everything under control. His thoughts are not our thoughts and his ways are not our ways. He has perfect timing for the manifestation of His will for our lives. Jeremiah 29:11 confirms it, "I know the thoughts and the plans that I have for you, says GOD. Thoughts and plans of peace and not of evil to give you an expected end." Psalm 46:10 tells us to be still and know that I am God. With that in mind, calm down and enjoy the journey!

PRINCIPLE TWO: STAND IN FAITH!

Roman 1:17 declares that the just shall live by faith. This is not an option. If you're in the kingdom of God, you have to live by faith. You are not always going to see it in your hand but you have to see it in your spirit. Hebrews 4:2 says the message that they heard profited them nothing because it was not mixed with faith. You have to hear the Word and then mix it with your faith because "now faith the substance of things hope for and the evidence of things not seen." When you, hear the word, apply it by faith to your life, allowing it to grow and take root in your life, you will see results. The Word of GOD will not return void but it will accomplish everything it was set out to do.

Mary made the decision that she was going to stand in faith. Mary teaches us to never try to explain or get people to understand the promise that God has made to us! Nowhere in the text do you see Mary trying to explain why she had been chosen for the promise. She knew what Gabriel had spoken to her and that was all she cared about. Therefore, she was able to stand in faith. The message is crystal clear here. Stop spending your time trying to justify and explain to people about your promise. When it comes to standing in faith, ask yourself, "Am I more dedicated to the distractions in my life or my destiny?" For your sake, I hope you have made a decision to stand in faith and believe GOD for your promise. Don't let distractions get you so off focus that you lose heart and give up on the dream seed inside of you.

PRINCIPLE THREE: STUDY TO BE QUIET!

1 Thessalonians 4:11 tells us to study to be quiet. Oftentimes, we talk too much and too long to the wrong people. When you believe God for something, you have to be strategic in what you let come out of your mouth. In Luke 1:34, Mary was getting analytical when she said, "How can this be, when I have not known a man." Like Mary, how many times have we talked ourselves out of a miracle, out of a blessing or out of a breakthrough because we were so busy looking at things in the natural, which caused us to doubt the power of GOD? For this reason, we have to be mindful of what we allow to lay dormant in our minds because eventually that stuff comes out of our mouths.

The bible tells us to cast down every imagination and high thing that exalts itself against the knowledge of GOD. Don't allow the natural part of you to override the supernatural part of you. The carnal mind will never understand spiritual things. Guard your mouth and your heart! Your mouth has the power to either resuscitate (cause things to come back to life) or to kill. This is why we have to be careful of how we communicate. Your words can either build things up or tear them down. Your words have the ability to penetrate hearts, change minds and create an atmosphere that is conducive for miracles to take place. The bible says that you can decree a thing and it shall be established. Don't allow your flesh or your analytical mind to get you to speak against the promise you believe God for!

PRINCIPLE FOUR: WORK!

James 2:20 tells us that faith without works is dead. After having made a decision to stand in faith, you have to be willing to do some work. The Lord will bless your efforts with good success. Habakkuk 2:2 says, "Write the vision and make it plain." The set time is now to plan your work and work your plan. Nothing just happens! Oprah Winfrey said, "Success happens when an opportunity meets a prepared person." You have a responsibility to do the work required so you can not only obtain the promise but be in a position to maintain it. Indeed, the blessings of the LORD make you rich and add no sorrow.

You are required to have the confidence to work towards a goal and stick to it until it comes to pass. I want to remind you that if you can see it, believe it, because you can achieve it! Work for it! GOD Himself gave you the dream seed! He would not have given it to you if it was not possible.

PRINCIPLE FIVE: BEWARE OF YOUR SURROUNDINGS!

In Luke 1:41, Mary was strategic with who she was hanging out with. She went to Elisabeth's house and as soon as Mary spoke, the baby within Elisabeth began to leap. In this season, it is of the utmost importance that you evaluate the company that you keep.

There are four types of people in the world: The Adder's, the Subtracter's, the Multiplier's, and the Divider's. The Adder's are the positive people that add to your life. The Subtracter's are the leeches, parasites, and ticks that are always taking away from you instead of adding to you. The Divider's are the ones that always want to break you down until you are at your lowest. They can not see past where they are. So, they want to rob you of your vision. The Multiplier's are the people that seem to stir you up on the inside when you are around them. They start giving your faith a boost. They just have a way of stimulating your thinking. They challenge you to think outside of the box and help you to develop a strategic plan on how to make all of your dreams a reality! My imagination needs the stimulation of the association of successful others. Evaluate your surroundings and don't be afraid to cut the sucka's loose. If they can't help you, please don't allow people to stick around and rob you mentally and rape you spiritually! Cut them OFF!

PRINCIPLE SIX: POSITION YOURSELF!

When desiring to birth out the promises of God, you have to make sure that you are in the right position. What I mean is that you have to make sure that you are in right standing with God. Deuteronomy tells us if you will be willing and obedient, you shall eat the good of the land. Even if you find yourself in a back-slidden state or perhaps never knew Jesus as Lord, there is still hope for you. According to I John 1:9, "If you confess your sins, he is faithful and just to forgive you of your sins and cleanse you from all unrighteousness." The set time is now to position yourself to receive the promises of God concerning you.

PRINCIPLE SEVEN: FIGHT FOR IT!

We all know that the devil is a serial killer. He comes to kill, still, and destroy. He wants nothing more than to gain the victory over you at a vulnerable time in your life. Especially when you are in the position to receive all that has been promised to you. Matthew 16:19 informs you that you have been given keys to the kingdom. Whatsoever you bind on earth shall be bound in heaven and whatever you loose on earth shall be loosed in heaven. You have to know that the kingdom of heaven suffers violence and the violent have to take it by force. You've got to fight for it!

Now is not the time to get scared. It is time for you to fight the good fight of faith, knowing that God has given you power and authority over the enemy. When you are fighting for your promise, you need to be prepared to engage in spiritual warfare. Put on the whole armor of God so that you can stand against the wiles of the devil. For the weapons of your warfare are not carnal but mighty through God to the pulling down of strongholds. You wrestle not against flesh and blood but against spiritual wickedness in high places. So, you have to take authority and FIGHT for your promise!

PRINCIPLE EIGHT: PUSH!

In Luke 2, you will note that Mary had to push her way through some issues to birth the promised child. Mary shows us the importance of having endurance and resilience. She had the ability to push through the pain and discomfort of having had her organs shifted from one position to another to house the promise of GOD. She endured the nine months of emotional roller-coasters, swollen feet, etc. that come along with pregnancy for the benefit of all mankind.

Isaiah 9:6 6, "For unto us a child is born, unto us a son is given: and the government shall be upon his shoulder: and his name shall be called Wonderful, Counselor, The mighty God, The everlasting Father, The Prince of Peace." Like Mary, you too have to have a made up mind that you are going to push your way through whatever you have to in order to receive your promise. Some days you may have to **P**ray-**U**ntil-**S**omething-**H**appens! You might have to **P**reach-**U**ntil-**S**omething-**H**appens! You might have to be like Ezekiel and say can these dry bones live and begin to **P**rophesy-**U**ntil-**S**omething-**H**appens! I dare you to start prophesying to your situation! Speak life! For life and death is in the power of your tongue. Last but not least, like Mary, Praise-Until-Something-Happens! Mary said my soul does magnify the Lord. To magnify means to enlarge; to see bigger. Can you see God bigger than your circumstance today? If you do, then you can continue to Praise-Until- Something-Happens!

A promise is a promise. You serve a GOD that can not lie! His Word will not return unto Him void but it will accomplish everything that He set it out to do. Your praise is the spiritual epidural that makes waiting for the manifestation a little easier! Make it up in your mind, "I will bless the LORD at all times and his praise shall continue to be in my mouth!"

A PROMISE IS STILL A PROMISE

You may be broke on today. Perhaps, you have been laid off from your job and you don't know how you are going to make it. I want you to know there is a promise for that situation: Psalm 37:25, "I have been young, and now am old; yet have I not seen the righteous forsaken, nor his seed begging bread." Philippians 4:19 says "But my God shall supply all of your needs according to his riches in glory by Christ Jesus." Perhaps, your body is under attack. Praise Him for the promise found in Isaiah 53:5, "But he was wounded for our transgressions, he was bruised for our iniquities: the chastisement of our peace was upon him; and with his stripes we are healed." and the promise that is found in Psalm 103:3 "Who forgiveth all thine iniquities; who healeth all thy diseases;" Psalm 118:17 says, "I shall not die, but live, and declare the works of the LORD."

When you work the Word, the promises found in the Word of God will work for you! God still keeps His promises. His ability to manifest the promises in your life is not dependent upon what is going on right now. The Word says that it does not yet appear what you shall be. The grass may whither and the flowers my fade away but the Word of God will stand forever! God's promises do not have an expiration date! God keeps his PROMISES!

6

THE AMAZON RIVER - "RELATIONSHIPS"

I HAVE A FATHER!

Psalm 27:10
10 When my father and my mother forsake me, then the LORD will take me up.

Billy Graham once said, "A good father is one of the most unsung, unpraised, unnoticed, yet valuable assets in our society." At present, we live in a time where it is true that the value of a father has depreciated. Could it be a direct result of many people's constant struggle with their "daddy issues"? Issues of rejection, abandonment and low self-esteem have held so many people hostage to their pasts. Research studies have noted that over *70% of all persons involved in the criminal justice system come from fatherless homes.* While mothers all across this world have worked diligently to provide and protect their children, it still does not replace the presence of a father.

On today, you may feel a bit depressed, thinking about what you never had in a father. The good news is that you have a father! In our text, we find in Psalms 27:10 that you have been adopted into the kingdom. Your relationship with the Father GOD can at times be imitated but never can His presence in your life be duplicated! He is the only man I know that promises never to leave you or forsake you. He was there in the good times, he was there in the bad and rest assured, he will be with you until the end of times! Father God has never been issued an OFA (order for arrest) for being behind on child support. He is known by many as Jehovah-Jireh, your Provider; AKA El-Shaddai, the all- sufficient One, who promised to supply all of your needs according to His riches and GLORY! Oh, yes, you have a Father! There are so many qualities to describe His character and His personality. He is reliable and faithful according to Heb. 10:23, "Let us hold fast the profession of our faith without wavering." For, He is faithful. In addition, He is trustworthy according to Kings 8:56, "Blessed be the LORD, which hath given rest unto his people Israel, according to all that he promised: there hath not failed one word of all his good promise, which he promised by the hand of Moses his servant." That's good news! If He said it, His Word will never fail. Trust Him. He is trustworthy!

In conclusion, there are so many other things I could say about the Father but I want to leave you with this final thought. He is ever-loving and supportive. Jer. 31:3: "³The LORD hath appeared of old unto me, saying, Yea, I have loved thee with an everlasting love: therefore with loving-kindness have I drawn thee." Isa 41:10: "¹⁰Fear thou not; for I am with thee: be not dismayed; for I am thy God: I will strengthen thee; yea, I will help thee; yea, I will uphold thee with the right hand of my righteousness." Be encouraged on today that you have a Father who sits high and looks low. He is concerned about everything that concerns you. Trust Him with your life. Trust Him with your issues. He is waiting. Rev. 3:20 informs you that He stands there at the door of your heart, knocking and seeking the opportunity to enter and serve as your Father.

NOT YOUR AVERAGE WOMAN!

2 Peter 2:9
"But ye are a chosen generation, a royal priesthood, an holy nation, a peculiar people; that ye should shew forth the praises of him who hath <u>called</u> you out of darkness into his marvelous light;"

Mark 11:24
"Therefore I say unto you, Whatsoever things you desire when you pray, believe that you receive them and ye shall have them."

Many beautiful women who have graced the red carpets of Hollywood have been noted for their beauty, stylish flare and have been granted the status of being a label-wearing DIVA. However, the truth is beauty alone does not determine your true worth and value. Beautiful women are given platforms to air their dirty laundry on national TV all the time. They seemingly become famous for their behaviors, which oftentimes don't reflect who they really are as women. These reality shows may be entertaining but too often they discount the true essence, style, grace, and finesse required to be a peculiar woman; a woman who has been set apart, chosen and different from the "average" woman. Average women seem to just fit in and go with the flow. You, my sister, were never meant to fit in. Your presence demands attention because of the greater One that lives on the inside of you.

In August of 2009, I had the awesome opportunity to meet a phenomenal man by the name of Joseph Washington, who wrote the book titled, **"Breaking the Spirit of Average"**. I found the principles in this book to be life-changing. Did you know that average is simply being the top of the bottom and the bottom of the top? It is a pain-killer that lulls you to sleep and gets you comfortable with just enough so you never reach for anything greater. A wise man once said, "Blessed are those that seek nothing; for they will never be disappointed!" I want to challenge you ladies to ask yourself if you had to be who you are today for the rest of your life, would you be happy? Have you lived your best life? Only you can give an account of what you have or have not accomplished with the time you have been given here on earth.

Oftentimes, we settle for being average. We put off our personal goals and dreams to make other people happy and we never take the time to really invest in ourselves. We fail to cultivate and develop the garden of possibilities on the inside of us, being so busy with the cares of this world. This is the very reason why the graveyard is said to be one of the riches place in the world. There are many bodies there of people who never wrote the books, started the businesses, etc.

Don't let fear stop you from living your best and being your best! There will always be people who will sit and watch and criticize others and question WHY? We, as children of God and peculiar people must become the generation that looks at things that have never been done and say, why not. Always reach for the moon. You're destined to land among the stars! When you believe, really believe something can be done, your mind will find ways to do it! Mark 11:24 gives us a simple but practical recipe for receiving from GOD. Establish and maintain a desire, pray, making your requests known to GOD and finally, believe and you will receive. You are not an Average Woman. You're a Woman of Purpose; a Woman full of divine possibilities! Believe in yourself. Believe in your ability. Believe that you can succeed in all that you put your hand to do. I BELIEVE IN YOU, MY SISTER! You are not an average woman.

THE COMPANY THAT YOU KEEP

1 Cor. 15:33:
"Bad Company corrupts good manners."

Allow me to start this section with a question. "ARE YOU MORE DEDICATED TO THE DISTRACTIONS IN YOUR LIFE OR YOUR DESTINY? Without thinking, we often entertain and interact with people. Life is built upon the premise that no man is an island and that we need each other to survive. In the text, I Cor. 15:33, "Bad company corrupts good manners." It is crystal clear that everyone who enters your life has your best interest in mind but can possibly run the risk of contaminating you and or causing unnecessary chaos. In this case, these people are considered to be a distraction. If you are not careful, these individuals will cause irritation and frustration to the point that you loose sight of your purpose and destiny. While I am not encouraging you to become judgmental, I am encouraging you to establish yourself as a fruit inspector. The Bible says that you will know them by the fruit that they bear. In this day and time, you have to be wise about who you allow to occupy space in your sphere of influence.

The bible tells us to be as wise as a serpent and as humble as a dove. If an individual in your life is bearing fruit that is not productive but rather counter-productive to the plan and purpose God has for your life, you may need to consider your ways. It's funny how the world has established all kinds of assessments and personality tests in hope of helping you to identify your personality and the most effective way to interact with each other in the workplace. Unlike those various scientific-research based evaluations, I have established a simple way of evaluating the types of people in the world. It's as simple as elementary mathematics. In this world, there are four types of people: ADDER'S, SUBTRACTER'S, MULTIPLER'S and DIVIDER'S.

The Adder's are the positive people in your life that typically have pleasant, uplifting things to say. They tend to have an overall positive outlook on life. On the other hand, the Subtracter's are similar to that of leeches, parasites and ticks. These individuals often have a very negative frame of reference. They seem to never have anything positive to say. In addition, they lack the ability to give. A relationship with a Subtracter is typically one-sided. You give and they receive. The Divider's are very similar to that of the Subtracter but on a greater scale. This type of person will find a way to break you down to your lowest common denominator. Have you ever had a conversation with someone and by the time the conversation was over, you found yourself drained? If so, you may be entertaining a Divider. Last but not least is the Multiplier. This is the kind of person that always seems to stir you up on the inside. They seem to find a way to bring out the best in you. After having encountered a Multiplier, you are motivated, inspired, and empowered to be your best self!

In closing, you only have one life to live. It is your responsibility to take care of yourself and to guard your heart! Seek God and trust Him to surround you with the right people. Consider the Company that you Keep!

DATING: 101

Prov 19: 2 Also, that the soul be without knowledge, it is not good; and he that hasteth with his feet sinneth.
Proverbs 16:3 Commit thy works unto the LORD, and thy thoughts shall be established.
Isa 26:3 Thou wilt keep him in perfect peace, whose mind is stayed on thee: because he trusteth in thee.

Webster's dictionary defines the term single as not being married; not accompanied by others; solitary. Being single and the process of dating is no easy task. Some tend view the state of singleness like that of the latter part of the definition-solitary confinement. They then get in a hurry to get married without doing the proper preparation. Therefore, they end up married and miserable.

Staying focused as a single man or woman in the kingdom is not always an easy thing to do. The spirit is willing but the flesh is weak! Below are some key principles to empower you to make right decisions as you engage in what I call Dating 101. As you embark upon the process of dating, keep in mind that dating is the process of collecting data. Some would describe singleness as the process chamber, in which God purifies, perfects, develops and then gives birth to that which is on the inside of you. It's important to stay in the process chamber and not allow yourself to be distracted. A distraction is anything or anybody that interrupts your purpose and destiny.

PRINCIPLE #1: GUARD YOUR HEART & KNOW WHO YOU ARE DEALING WITH.

The bible tells us to be very careful about giving away our affections because our heart influences everything else in our lives. Proverbs 4:23 states, "above all else, guard your heart, for it is the wellspring of life." Before you open up yourself to heartbreak, take the time to really get to know the person; not just their representative. Ask yourself, what kind of reputation does my potential date have? Will there be any pressure to compromise my integrity? Will this date put a damper on my ministry, or send mix messages to others we come in contact with?

In the event you find that you are constantly attracting the wrong type of person in your life, consider the message that you are sending. In addition it's important to keep in mind that your anointing will attract individuals who may be attracted to you for ministry purpose. Every individual who enters your life is not a candidate for dating. Guard your heart and remain prayerful, God will let you know who and what your dealing with. Don't allow your emotions and impatience to have you in hurry and making irrational decisions.

Proverb 11:14 safety in a multitude of counsel. It is important that you surround yourself with real friends who will tell you the truth in love.... Not just about what you're wearing or how your hair looks, but the truth about the person that you're dating. Sometime we get blinded by their looks and what we perceive as a great benefit that we can't see the warning signs of danger!!! This is where real friends, not haters or folks that are jealous of you come in, who will tell you the truth and pray for you! You got to have somebody you can trust! As singles we need accountability partners to help us on our journey!

PRINCIPLE #2: BEWARE: LOVE SHOULD NOT HURT!

First of all it is important to get a clear understanding of the term love. Sometimes as singles we have been guilty of being in love with the thought of being in love, but what is love? 1 Corinthians

13:4-7 defines real love for us. When considering the topic of love in dating, ask yourself these questions:

1. Are you patient with each other?
2. Are you kind to each other?
3. Are you never envious of each other?
4. Do you never boast to or about each other?
5. Is your relationship characterized by humility?
6. Are you never rude to each other?
7. Are you not self-seeking?
8. Are you not easily angered with each other?
9. Do you keep no record of wrongs?
10. Are you truthful with each other?
11. Do you protect each other?
12. Do you trust each other?

If you answered "yes" to the above questions, then 1 Corinthians 13 says that you truly have a loving relationship. If you answered "no" to any of the above questions, then maybe you should discuss those issues with your significant other. Many persons tend to stay stuck in unhealthy relationships and find themselves abused physically, and or emotionally. Love should not hurt! No where in this text has love been described as a painfully emotion. The bible instructs us in Proverbs 16:3 to commit our works to the LORD, and its then and only then will we be established.

It's also important to note that many people tend to stay in toxic relationships due to soul ties. Soul ties are real and can contribute to the ongoing pattern and cycle of hurt & pain in a relationships. A soul tie is the deep bond that is developed between two or more individuals through an unhealthy relationship leading to addictive, manipulative or even violent behavior. When there is a soul tie in relationships outside marriage, you can hear people say things like, "I can't live without you, I can't be happy without you" or "I will die without you". These relationships are not based on the spirit's love, peace and joy. These soul ties can lead to domestic violence, and what some refer to as the stalker mentality.

In the event you find that you have a soul tie, be confident that deliverance is yours for the asking. First of all you must identify where you have opened the door to the enemy in your life. Denounce that relationship, those behaviors and totally surrender your life to Jesus and let him rule over your soul. Take time to pray and confess the word of God over your life and begin to fill your mind with the things of GOD rather than playing the mental tapes over and over again in your mind from the past. For some, you may have to throw away everything that reminds you of the past and/or keeps you mentally and emotionally attached. Beware my brothers and sisters – Love should not hurt!

PRINCIPLE #3: KNOW YOUR WORTH AND VALUE, THEN DETERMINE WHAT YOU WANT.

It is of utmost importance that you understand your own worth and value. You are a priceless jewel that has been fearfully and wonderfully made in the image of GOD. You are not damaged goods! When people don't realize their worth, their self esteem tends to be very low and they tend to just settle for who and what comes along. You don't have to do that; you can ask for whatsoever you want from GOD. The bible speaks about making your request known unto GOD. It is your responsibility to decide what you want in a potential mate and submit these requests to GOD. Matt 6:33 states, "Seek first the kingdom of God and his righteousness and all these things will be added unto you." Mark 11:24 states, "whatsoever things you desire when you pray believe that you receive and you shall have them." We can believe God for everything else, why can't we use the same faith and believe God for our desires in a mate. In addition determine your deal breakers and don't settle. The use of a vision board can be used to keep your vision and desires fresh before you. Also this can serve as a check list to evaluate the person of interest, if they don't fit you must acquit.

In conclusion, stay at peace in your singleness no matter what. Be confident that the blessings of the Lord will indeed make you rich and add no sorrow, and that does include a mate. When you seek him first according to Matt 6:33, God will take pleasure in blessing you! He wants to give you the very desires of our hearts. You must trust him even if you can not trace him, for his ways are always perfect. While your waiting on the manifestation of what you have requested from GOD, enjoy the journey. Take the time to build a personal relationship with God & yourself, you are complete in HIM! Your labor will not be in vain. I'm believing GOD for you and your hearts desire for a mate. May the GOD of peace give you your hearts desires and bless you in such a mighty way that you forget all about who & what that did not work in the past because the blessings of the Lord according to Deu. 28 has come upon you and has overtaken you! You are worth it, walk in it!

SINGLE AFTER GOD'S OWN HEART

I Cor. 7:34 -35
34There is difference also between a wife and a virgin. The unmarried woman careth for the things of the Lord, that she may be holy both in body and in spirit: but she that is married careth for the things of the world, how she may please her husband. 35And this I speak for your own profit; not that I may cast a snare upon you, but for that which is comely, and that ye may attend upon the Lord without **distraction.**

The stigma associated with being an unmarried person in our society often gives the perception that being single is bad. On today I want to encourage you that being single is not a curse, as a matter of fact it is a blessing. It all boils down to your perception.

As a single individual you have been granted the opportunity to fulfill your purpose in the earth without distractions. At times we can get to frustrated by our marital status that we fail to identify our purpose, the very thing we were created for, because we are so focus on a significant other. There is so much more to you, you are filled with so much potential to do great things. Don't allow your focus to be just on getting married.

My question to you today is simply this, are you more dedicated to the distractions in your life or your destiny? Allow me to warn you, the enemy has studied you; he knows exactly what you like and will do whatever necessary to get you off focus with distractions! For that reason you must guard your heart, and focus on the things of God.

Below are some power principles I have used to personally overcome the sigma of merely existing as a single woman and becoming a single woman after Gods own heart. You can live an awesome single life!

S-SURRENDER TO THE WILL OF GOD
I-IDENTIFY YOUR PURPOSE
N-NEVER UNDER ESTIMATE THE FLESH
G-GIVE GOD SOME QUALITYTIME
L-LIVE BY THE WORD
E-ENLIST THE HELP OF MENTORS
L-LAUGH OFTEN
I-INVEST TIME IN HELPING OTHERS
F-FACE YOUR FEARS WITH FAITH
E-EMPOWER YOUR BELIEF SYSTEM

ABOUT THE AUTHOR:

Kendra is an active member of Greater Cleveland Avenue Christian Church, where Bishop Sheldon M. McCarter is Senior Pastor. In November of 2005 Kendra was licensed as a minister of the Gospel. Since that time, she was ordained as an Elder. Her labor of love speaks for itself. She has worked diligently in the kingdom and has made full proof of her ministry gift according to 2 Timothy 4: 1-5 & the ability to carry out the great commission.

In addition to preaching the gospel as opportunity presents, she serves as a spiritual sniper in the area of Deliverance Ministry and Spiritual Warfare. She is a powerful Intercessory Prayer Warrior, Alter Worker, and member of the Outreach & Prison Ministry. Her life work has been committed to empowering individuals to live the kind of life that Jesus died for them to have.

Kendra is a 1999 & 2009 graduate of Winston-Salem State University, where she earned both a Bachelor of Science Degree in Sociology (1999) & a Master of Science Degree in Rehabilitation Counseling (2009). She is a licensed Substance Abuse Counselor and Certified Criminal Justice Addiction Professional. She is also certified by the National Association of Forensic Counselors as a Certified Sex Offender Treatment Specialist.

In October of 2009, the Winston-Salem Chronicle featured an article reflecting the life changing work of Kendra Davis at the Forsyth Correctional Center, where she was responsible for the development & implementation of a rehabilitation / re-entry program for current adult inmates and recently released offenders who desire to break the cycle of crime and punishment.
While counseling individuals with substance abuse disorders, sex offenders and those who are currently incarcerated are her area of expertise, she has also worked in other positions in the community

throughout her career that reflect her character as a "true humanitarian".

In 2010, Kendra established K*METAMORPHOSIS, a Christian counseling organization whose vision, mission and philosophy was birthed out of the desire to fill a much needed treatment gap in the community. The organization's mission is to utilize a holistic approach to restore fallen humanity. This organization was built on the belief, that individuals like that of a caterpillar, who at one time did not look like very much, limited by his surroundings and lifestyle on the ground, but after having gone through a process called "metamorphosis", his life changed drastically! With that in mind this organization believes that individuals are capable of changing from the inside out and will successfully transitioning from one phase in their life to another. This organization is committed to empower individuals with the necessary tools, including the word of GOD to recover with dignity and respect.

Kendra's motto: "Your past failures will not dictate your future, or hold you hostage unless you allow it!""God will give beauty for ashes...(Isa. 61:3). Knowing that the suffering of this present time is not worthy to be compared to the glory that shall be revealed (Rom. 8:18). Because better is the end of a thing than the beginning thereof (Ecc. 7:8)

To correspond with Elder Kendra T. Davis:

Kendra Davis Ministries
P.O. Box 663
Winston-Salem, NC 27102

Email her at info@kendradavis.com

Or log on to her website at:

www.kendradavis.com

For booking information:

336-422-PRAY (7729)

Or log on to
www.kendradavis.com